Why Was Billy Bunter Never Really Expelled?

Why Was Billy Bunter Never Really Expelled?

And Another Twenty-Five Mysteries of Children's Literature

Dennis Butts and Peter Hunt

The Lutterworth Press

The Lutterworth Press
P.O. Box 60
Cambridge
CB1 2NT
United Kingdom

www.lutterworth.com
publishing@lutterworth.com

Paperback ISBN: 978 0 7188 9544 0
PDF ISBN: 978 0 7188 4790 6
ePub ISBN: 978 0 7188 4791 3
Kindle ISBN: 978 0 7188 4792 0

British Library Cataloguing in Publication Data
A record is available from the British Library

First published by The Lutterworth Press, 2019
Copyright © Dennis Butts and Peter Hunt, 2019

Cover images:
John Tenniel, 'The White Rabbit', illustration for *Alice's Adventures in Wonderland* (1865); Enrico Mazzanti, coloured by Daniel Donna, 'Pinocchio', illustration for *Le avventure di Pinocchio: Storia di un burattino* (1883); Randalf Caldecott, 'And the Dish Ran Away with the Spoon', illustration from 'Hey Diddle Diddle' and 'Bye, Baby Bunting' (George Routledge and Sons, 1882); Walter Crane, 'The better to see you with', woodcut for 'Little Red Riding Hood' (1875).

All rights reserved. No part of this edition may be reproduced, stored electronically or in any retrieval system, or transmitted in any form or by any means, electronic, mechanical, photocopying, recording, or otherwise, without prior written permission from the Publisher (permissions@lutterworth.com).

Contents

List of Illustrations	ix
Introduction	xi

1. Should Children Read Fairy Tales?   1
   DENNIS BUTTS

2. What Makes a Children's Classic?   6
   PETER HUNT

3. Why Were there no Nursery Rhymes before 1744?   12
   Tom Thumb's Pretty Song Book, Vol. II
   DENNIS BUTTS

4. Who Wrote *Little Goody Two-Shoes*?   18
   Little Goody Two-Shoes (1765)
   DENNIS BUTTS

5. What (and Where) Are the Secret, Lost Books of Childhood   23
   – and Why Do They Matter?
   PETER HUNT

6. The Curious History of Three Bears . . . and a Lamb   31
   'Goldilocks and the Three Bears' and 'Mary had a Little Lamb'
   DENNIS BUTTS

7. Charles Kingsley: Christian Socialist, Evangelical Storyteller,   35
   or Sexual Sadist?
   The Water-Babies (1863)
   DENNIS BUTTS

8. Who Was the Real William Brighty Rands? 40
   Lilliput Levee (1864)
   DENNIS BUTTS

9. Why Are there so many Dead Parents in Children's Books? 46
   PETER HUNT

10. Was Lorna Doone really Married? 52
    R.D. Blackmore, *Lorna Doone* (1869)
    DENNIS BUTTS

11. Whatever Happened to God in Children's Books? 56
    From *The History of the Fairchild Family* to
    Harry Potter and the Philosopher's Stone
    PETER HUNT

12. Whose Side Was Henty really on in the American Civil War? 63
    G.A. Henty, *With Lee in Virginia: A Story of the American Civil War* (1895)
    DENNIS BUTTS

13. What Do Children's Books Do about Christmas? 68
    PETER HUNT

14. Is *Little Lord Fauntleroy* a Children's Story – and Does 74
    the Subplot Work?
    Frances Hodgson Burnett, *Little Lord Fauntleroy* (1886)
    DENNIS BUTTS

15. Why Was Billy Bunter never really Expelled from 79
    Greyfriars School?
    The Magnet (1908-40)
    DENNIS BUTTS

16. Why on Earth Are there Children's Books about War? 84
    PETER HUNT

17. Biggles: Tough Guy or Romantic Hero? 91
    W.E. Johns, *The Camels Are Coming* (1932), *Biggles Buries a Hatchet* (1958), and *Biggles Looks Back* (1965)
    DENNIS BUTTS

18. Why Is there Nobody Nice at St Clare's? 94
    Enid Blyton, *The O'Sullivan Twins* (1947)
    PETER HUNT

Contents

19. Were there Two Flutes? Time Present and Time Past   101
    at Green Knowe
    L.M. Boston, *The Children of Green Knowe* (1954)
    DENNIS BUTTS

20. Why Does C.S. Lewis Annoy so many People?   106
    The Chronicles of Narnia (1950-6)
    PETER HUNT

21. What Happened Next? The Problem of Sequels   114
    DENNIS BUTTS

22. To See Ourselves . . . What Image of the British   120
    Do Children's Books Give the World?
    PETER HUNT

23. Why Is there no such Thing as Children's Poetry?   128
    Ted Hughes and Michael Rosen
    PETER HUNT

24. Which Are the Best 100 Children's Books?   135
    DENNIS BUTTS

25. And Which Is *the* Best?   140
    The Carnegie Medal and other Awards
    PETER HUNT

26. A Mystery Solved: How Adults Read Children's Books   146
    PETER HUNT

Notes   157

Index   163

List of Illustrations

The History of Jack and the Giants	2
Gustave Doré's 'Little Red Riding Hood' (1883)	5
J.M. Dent's 'Children's Illustrated Classics' series (1950s)	7
Mary Cooper's *Tommy Thumb's Pretty Song Book, Volume II* (1744)	13
Chapbook from c. 1700	16
The History of Little Goody Two-Shoes (children's book publisher, John Newbery, 1766)	19
Betty Larom's *The Story of Baba* (1949)	25
Katharine Tozer's *Mumfie Marches On* (1942)	27
Joyce A. Johnson's illustration for Rosalind Vallance's *Timmy Turnpenny* (1937)	29
One of the sketches made by Charles Kingsley for his future wife, Fanny (1843)	37
William Brighty Rands: from an 1899 edition of *Lilliput Lyrics* illustrated by Charles Robinson	41
Sara and Emily in Frances Hodgson Burnett's fist version of *A Little Princess, Sara Crewe or What Happened at Miss Minchin's* (1888) illustrated by Reginald B. Birch	47

Doone Valley, Exmoor, Devon	53
Judy rushes to her death in Ethel M. Turner's *Seven Little Australians* (1894); illustration by A.J. Johnson	57
Blackie's flyer for G.A. Henty (1867)	64
Thomas Nast's 'Merry Old Santa' (1881)	69
Illustration by Reginald B. Birch for Frances Hodgson Burnett's *Little Lord Fauntleroy* (1886)	75
Billy Bunter illustrated by Charles Henry Chapman between 1911 and the 1970s	80
The Greyfriars chums, from a souvenir edition of 1965	83
Dangerously unrealistic version of war from the prolific Percy F. Westerman (1917)	85
Some of Biggles's First World War exploits, first published in 1934, and reissued in the 1970s	92
The School Friend in 1936 with a guest appearance by Bessie Bunter, Billy's sister	95
Alias 'Green Knowe': the ancient and atmospheric Manor at Hemingford Grey, on the Great Ouse near Huntingdon	103
C.S. Lewis (1898-1963), photograph courtesy of Steven A. Beebe	107
Samuel Goodrich's *The Tales of Peter Parley About America* (1828)	115
John Tenniel's picture of Alice playing croquet in Lewis Carroll's *Alice's Adventures in Wonderland* (1865)	121
An illustration by Enrico Mazzanti for the first edition of Carlo Collodi's *Le avventure di Pinocchio* (1883)	125
Kathleen Lines's *Four to Fourteen* with an introduction by Walter de la Mare	137
Arthur Ransome (1884-1967)	147

Introduction

'Why does Edgar not reveal himself to his blind father, as he truly says that he ought to have done? The answer is left to mere conjecture.'
– A.C. Bradley on *King Lear*

When our little study on *How Did Long John Silver Lose his Leg? And Twenty-Six Other Mysteries of Children's Literature* appeared in 2013, instead of the storm of abuse we expected, the work was greeted, along with a few compliments, with a series of complaints and grumbles as to why other mysteries, which were of particular importance to the complainants, had not been tackled. The urge to speculate about various problems in children's books is evidently more widespread than we had anticipated.

This may be partly due to nostalgia, of course. Many of our readers urged us to investigate mysteries that had no doubt first occurred to them when thinking about their years of juvenile enthusiasms, perhaps after re-reading old favourites in middle age. Hence there were many queries about the Biggles books, about Richmal Crompton's great comedies involving William Brown, and concerning Frank Richards's immortal character, Billy Bunter. So here we attempt to tackle some of those queries, as well as to investigate other popular works, such as *Lorna Doone*; *The Lion, the Witch and the Wardrobe*; and Enid Blyton's school stories set at St Clare's.

Other chapters have a more theoretical base – about the problems of religion and of war in children's books, the difficulties of writing a series of books about the same characters, and about the long-running debate on the value of fairy tales. Others are more speculative – about questions of authorship, or of the challenge of deciding which children's books are 'classics', of trying to identify and list the 100 best children's books, or of trying to award prizes to the *very* best.

In many cases there are no definitive answers, of course. As A.C. Bradley, the great Shakespearian scholar, said in his essay upon *King Lear*, 'The answer is [often] left to mere conjecture.'

I.

Should Children Read Fairy Tales?

The answer seems obvious: 'They always have, and they always will.' But it is not quite that simple. To begin with, not many fairy tales were actually published before the eighteenth century – the phrase *fairy tale* itself only appeared for the first time in 1749 – and, even if they had been, not many children would have been able to read them. Romances, fables, and folktales, such as 'Jack the Giant Killer' were initially circulated orally, and from the 16th century in cheap pamphlets called chapbooks.

Compared with these literary genres, fairy tales are relatively modern. The earliest European storybooks to include fairy tales came from Italy in the sixteenth century, and the first collection to achieve world-wide impact was the *Histoires ou Contes du Temps Passé* by Charles Perrault (1628-1703) published in Paris in 1697, which was first translated into English in 1729. The success of this volume, which included such stories as 'The Sleeping Beauty', 'Little Red Riding Hood', and 'Cinderella', inspired other collectors and authors. The Brothers Grimm had their collection of German tales, including 'Snow White' and 'Hansel and Gretel', published as *German Popular Stories,* and these were translated into English by Edgar Taylor in 1823. A few years later the Danish author Hans Christian Andersen (1805-1875) published his *Tales for Children,* including 'The Tinder Box' and 'The Princess and the Pea', which were first translated into English in 1846. Such stories have been read and enjoyed by children and adults ever since.

But, it has to be pointed out, many of these tales, initially at any rate, may not have been written for children. Charles Perrault was a court official and member of the French Academy, and his tales are told in a

The History
of
Jack the Giant Killer

WITH MANY ENGRAVINGS

A NEW EDITION

Adapted for Juvenile Readers of the Present Day

1830

London :
Dean & Co., Threadneedle Street

Still violent after all these years:
a 17th century survival, originally *The History of Jack and the Giants*.

sophisticated language perhaps more designed to amuse the courtiers of Versailles than young children. The 'Morals' in verse at the end of each tale are rather more worldly and cynical than the pious precepts a child reader might expect. The Brothers Grimm were not writing for children either: Jacob (1785-1863) and Wilhelm (1786-1859) were philologists who collected old German tales for scholarly and historical purposes. Hans Christian Andersen is an even more ambiguous figure. He was not a collector of folktales like the Brothers Grimm, but a creative artist who used the form of fantasy and the fairy tale as a literary genre. He fought against his reputation as a kind of Pied Piper, saying that 'my tales were just as much for older people as for children, who only understood the outer trappings and did not comprehend and take in the whole work until they were mature'. This did not prevent Andersen's tales, such as 'The Little Match Girl' and 'The Ugly Duckling', from being read and admired by children all over the world.

But almost from the first publication serious doubts were expressed about the suitability of fairy tales for young readers. The Christian church, especially the seventeenth-century Puritans, regarded allusions to fairies and fairy land, which challenged ideas of Heaven and Hell, as almost blasphemous. In the eighteenth century even the great Maria Edgeworth (1767-1849), although herself a gifted story-teller for children, strongly disliked fairy tales, partly because of her insistence that stories ought to be based upon reason and probability rather than the imagination, and because she feared fairy tales failed to offer good moral examples for young, impressionable minds.

But the strongest opposition to fairy tales came at the beginning of the nineteenth century when Mrs Sarah Trimmer (1741-1810), a devout Christian who was deeply concerned about the education of children, produced a periodical, *The Guardian of Education* (1802-6). She was especially interested in children's reading, and in her magazine, amidst a wide survey of children's books and reviews of current publications, she launched a ferocious attack on fairy tales. Although confessing that she had enjoyed some in her youth, she said that she now realised how harmful these books really were. Her grounds for criticism are complex but passionately expressed. She denounces fairy tales for encouraging the imagination rather than cultivating understanding. She also says that they were frequently irrational and absurd, and that the stories promote improper behaviour such as envy, vanity, and jealousy. Lastly, she says they are not only disturbing but positively frightening.

Her review in 1805 of a new edition of *Nursery Tales*, which included 'Cinderella', 'Blue Beard', and 'Little Red Riding Hood', is a tour de force:

> We doubt not but that many beside ourselves can recollect, their horrors of imagination on reading that of 'Blue Beard', and the terrific impressions it left upon their minds. This is certainly a very improper tale for children. 'Cinderella' and 'Little Red Riding Hood' are perhaps merely absurd. But it is not on account of their subjects and language only that these Tales ('Blue Beard' at least) are exceptionable, another objection to them arises from the nature of their embellishments, consisting of coloured prints, in which the most striking incidents in the stories are placed before the eyes of the little readers in glaring colours. . . . In 'Blue Beard', for instance, the second plate represents the opening of the *forbidden closet*, in which appears, not only what the story describes, (which surely is *terrific enough*!) '*a floor clotted with blood, in which the bodies of several women were lying (the wives whom Blue Beard had married and murdered,*) but, *the flames of Hell* with *Devils* in frightful shapes, threatening the unhappy lady who had given way to her curiosity! . . . A moment's consideration will surely be sufficient to convince people of the least reflection, of the danger, as well as the impropriety, of putting such books as these into the hands of little children, whose minds are susceptible of every impression; and who from the liveliness of their imaginations are apt to convert into realities whatever forcibly strikes their fancy.

It is not altogether easy to dismiss Mrs Trimmer's anxieties. One can find books with less gruesome illustrations perhaps, but one cannot ignore altogether the physical cruelty found in such tales as Andersen's 'Little Mermaid', the parental child abuse in 'Hansel and Gretel', or the opportunistic materialism of 'Big Klaus and Little Klaus'. Many adults will have had doubts about the menace expressed in such films as Walt Disney's *Snow White and the Seven Dwarfs* (1938).

From the 1970s, furthermore, many feminists have focused their attention on fairy tales, arguing that they often portray their female heroines as stereotypes, either weakly passive and only interested in finding a wealthy prince, or alternatively cruel and treacherous. It is also suggested that the Brothers Grimm, for example, in collecting their tales, frequently modified their texts while editing them to elevate the behaviour of male characters and to throw blame on the conduct of women.

There have, of course, been plenty of supporters of the fairy tale right from the nineteenth century, when Charles Dickens in 'Frauds on the Fairies' of 1853 famously attacked attempts to bowdlerize the tales

1. Should Children Read Fairy Tales?

The stuff of nightmares:
Gustave Doré's 'Little Red Riding Hood' (1883).

for children, and argued that they were essentially pure and innocent. Coleridge, Wordsworth, G.K. Chesterton, and W.H. Auden amongst other poets and writers have praised them too. More recently educationalists and psychologists, such as Kornei Chukovsky (1882-1970), Bruno Bettelheim (1903-90), and Maria Tatar (b. 1945) have discussed the effects of reading fairy tales upon young children and have argued that these stories, far from being frightening and immoral, offer young readers positive ways of dealing with conflict, sadness, and even violence in real life. This is all heady stuff, of course. But it just shows that asking a simple question can often lead to complicated answers.

2.
What Makes a Children's Classic?

Let us begin with three genuine mysteries. Firstly, what do these books have in common? *To Kill a Mockingbird, The Hound of the Baskervilles, Wuthering Heights, Pride and Prejudice, Frankenstein, The Italian, Tales of Mystery and Terror, Jane Eyre, The Count of Monte Cristo, Oliver Twist, Wives and Daughters,* and *The Woman in Black*.

And the answer is *not* that they are all books for adults (although they are).

Secondly, where would you find these books grouped together? *Mr Rabbit and the Lovely Present, Wise Children, Redwall, Midnight's Children, The Story of Tracy Beaker, To the Lighthouse, The Escape to Wonderland Colouring Book,* and *Down There On a Visit*.

Or, in which universe are these characters living side by side? The Famous Five, Peter Rabbit, Biggles, Mary Lennox, Little Miss Bossy, and Alice (of Wonderland)?

The answer is, in effect, the same for all of them: they are all on current publishers' lists of 'Children's Classics' (the books in the second group are all from the same publisher). They raise some interesting questions about the idea of the 'classic'. How is it that the first group, all initially written for adults, and still likely to be appropriate for adults, has ended up on children's lists? The second group – consisting of some books written for adults, some for children, some serious, some ephemeral, one wordless – raises the question of what these books, all in the same category, can possibly have in common. And even if we level the playing field – all the characters in the third group are from books written for children – surely there is a difference in quality?

2. What Makes a Children's Classic?

TITLES IN THE C.I.C. SERIES OF ILLUSTRATED CLASSICS

'A series which, in its own range and class, is still without rivals.'
The Times Literary Supplement

Children's Illustrated Classics

Aesop: FABLES
Alcott: GOOD WIVES
Alcott: JO'S BOYS
Alcott: LITTLE MEN
Alcott: LITTLE WOMEN
Hans Andersen: FAIRY TALES
Ballantyne: THE CORAL ISLAND
Ballantyne: THE DOG CRUSOE
Baum: THE MARVELLOUS LAND OF OZ
Baum: THE WONDERFUL WIZARD OF OZ
Frances Browne: GRANNY'S WONDERFUL CHAIR
Burnett: LITTLE LORD FAUNTLEROY
Carroll: ALICE'S ADVENTURES IN WONDERLAND and THROUGH THE LOOKING-GLASS
Collodi: PINOCCHIO
Coolidge: WHAT KATY DID
Dodge: HANS BRINKER
Mrs Ewing: THE BROWNIES AND OTHER STORIES
Mrs Ewing: LOB LIE-BY-THE-FIRE and THE STORY OF A SHORT LIFE
The Brothers Grimm: FAIRY TALES
Hawthorne: TANGLEWOOD TALES
Hawthorne: A WONDER BOOK
Hughes: TOM BROWN'S SCHOOLDAYS
Ingelow: MOPSA THE FAIRY
Kingsley: THE HEROES
Kingsley: THE WATER-BABIES
Lagerlöf: THE WONDERFUL ADVENTURES OF NILS
(Not available in the U.S.A. in this edition)
Lagerlöf: THE FURTHER ADVENTURES OF NILS
(Not available in the U.S.A. in this edition)
Charles and Mary Lamb: TALES FROM SHAKESPEARE
Andrew Lang: ADVENTURES OF ODYSSEUS

Andrew Lang: PRINCE PRIGIO and PRINCE RICARDO
MacDonald: AT THE BACK OF THE NORTH WIND
MacDonald: THE LOST PRINCESS
MacDonald: THE PRINCESS AND CURDIE
MacDonald: THE PRINCESS AND THE GOBLIN
Marryat: CHILDREN OF THE NEW FOREST
Mrs Molesworth: THE CARVED LIONS
Mrs Molesworth: THE CUCKOO CLOCK
E. Nesbit: THE ENCHANTED CASTLE
E. Nesbit: THE HOUSE OF ARDEN
Carola Oman: ROBIN HOOD
Raspe: BARON MUNCHAUSEN and other Comic Tales from Germany
Anna Sewell: BLACK BEAUTY
Spyri: HEIDI
Stevenson: A CHILD'S GARDEN OF VERSES
Thackeray: THE ROSE AND THE RING and Dickens: THE MAGIC FISH-BONE
Twain: HUCKLEBERRY FINN
Twain: THE PRINCE AND THE PAUPER
Twain: TOM SAWYER
A. H. Watson: NURSERY RHYMES
Wilde: THE HAPPY PRINCE & OTHER STORIES
J. R. Wyss: SWISS FAMILY ROBINSON
Charlotte M. Yonge: THE LITTLE DUKE
A BOOK OF MYTHS
THE BOOK OF NONSENSE
THE BOOK OF VERSE FOR CHILDREN
(Not available in the U.S.A. in this edition)
FAIRY TALES FROM THE ARABIAN NIGHTS
FAIRY TALES OF LONG AGO
KING ARTHUR AND THE ROUND TABLE
MODERN FAIRY STORIES
TALES OF MAKE BELIEVE

Illustrated Classics for Older Readers

Blackmore: LORNA DOONE
Buchan: THE THIRTY-NINE STEPS
Bunyan: THE PILGRIM'S PROGRESS
Cervantes: DON QUIXOTE (Abridged)
Childers: THE RIDDLE OF THE SANDS
Defoe: ROBINSON CRUSOE (Slightly abridged)
Dickens: A CHRISTMAS CAROL, etc.
Green: THE TALE OF ANCIENT ISRAEL
Haggard: KING SOLOMON'S MINES
Hope: THE PRISONER OF ZENDA
Hope: RUPERT OF HENTZAU
London: THE CALL OF THE WILD
London: WHITE FANG
Longfellow: SONG OF HIAWATHA
Merriman: BARLASCH OF THE GUARD

Seton: THE TRAIL OF THE SANDHILL STAG
Stevenson: THE BLACK ARROW
Stevenson: KIDNAPPED
Stevenson: TREASURE ISLAND
Swift: GULLIVER'S TRAVELS (Three of the four journeys)
Verne: AROUND THE MOON
Verne: AROUND THE WORLD IN 80 DAYS
Verne: FROM THE EARTH TO THE MOON
Verne: JOURNEY TO THE CENTRE OF THE EARTH
Verne: TWENTY THOUSAND LEAGUES UNDER THE SEA
Jean Webster: DADDY-LONG-LEGS
TEN TALES OF DETECTION
THIRTEEN UNCANNY TALES

Published by J. M. Dent & Sons Ltd, Bedford Street, London WC2E 9HG
E. P. Dutton & Co. Inc., New York, U.S.A.

Establishing the canon:
J.M. Dent's 'Children's Illustrated Classics' series from the 1950s.

How these books are all called classics is a genuine mystery, as is the definition of a 'classic' itself, a term that is now merrily applied by marketing persons to, well, anything: fizzy drinks, bank accounts, crisps, cars, fashions, and so on. And it generally refers to the previous, just-out-of-date, or still-selling-despite-our-efforts version.

A cynic might say that in literature, classics are books that we think we ought to read – and, eventually, probably think that we *have* read. But identifying a specific book as classic because of what it actually *is* – that is to say, what is on the page – is another matter. A good many publishers and authors have chased the answer – and the wealth it would bring – down the centuries, but, as those lists prove, it is a fruitless exercise.

Books carrying the label 'classic' rarely have much in common in terms of style or content. Definitions that bring in value judgements, such as Margery Fisher's notion that classics 'must offer universal truths, universal values, to one generation after another, impermeable to the erosion of Time', flounder on undefinable terms. Victor Watson's idea may seem to be less vulnerable to criticism: 'The great children's classics are those books our national consciousness cannot leave alone. We keep remaking them and reading them afresh'. But readers – and national consciousnesses – can only react to what is presented to them. Books may end up as being famous for being famous, and somebody must start the snowball rolling.

We might even conclude that publishers publish books labelled as 'classics' because most of those books are old and therefore out of copyright. The ones that aren't may be more recent books that happen to be published by the same publisher – thus prolonging the book's shelf-life. This is not as cynical as it sounds. The idea of producing series of 'classics' dates from the depression years in the USA, as Leonard S. Marcus explains:

> Classics in new or revived editions enjoyed renewed attention from publishers and readers alike. By reissuing books already in the public domain, publishers were able to factor out royalty payments from the cost side of the equation and thus to offer the books at more affordable prices.

In England, Methuen tried to capture the school literature market by launching Methuen Modern Classics in 1924, drawing on their backlist (*The Wind in the Willows* was one of the first titles – and one of the unabridged ones, as Grahame refused to allow anyone to take scissors to his work!). Dent followed, and now there is hardly a publisher or retailer that does not have a list of children's classics: currently, or in recent memory, we

2. What Makes a Children's Classic?

have seen Puffin Classics, Puffin Modern Classics, Young Puffin Modern Classics, Vintage, Red Fox, Oxford, Everyman, Ladybird, and on and on. 'Classics', then, either save publishers money or keep books from their backlists alive.

Regrettable as it may be in principle, all of this makes life rather easier for the majority of us who do not know much about children's books (and, let's face it, for people running children's book courses: it is easier to teach books that are widely available, thereby increasing the likelihood that their students might have read them). Furthermore, most people have a nostalgic or vague memory of books they encountered as children, and the classics lists are likely to have a book that stirs a chord (however out of tune). At least if we choose a 'classic' then we don't need to worry about our lack of expertise – the book must have the imprimatur of *somebody*.

Which is all very well, but there are obvious problems – notably the gap between the commercial instincts of the publishers and the needs of the young readers. I distinctly – vividly – remember an incident in my local children's bookshop a few years ago. A father and daughter came in – the daughter about ten years old – and she went immediately to the young adult section, while the father, rather uncertainly, browsed among the classics and found a copy of *Heidi*, complete with a cover of a small girl in a white frock on a flower-covered hillside. (It could have been in any of a dozen 'classic' editions.) The daughter, meanwhile had found, as I recall, the fourth volume in a series featuring teenage vampires, and there ensued an increasingly high-pitched negotiation that ended with both books being bought, on the condition that both were read. I had some sympathy with both participants: to one, *Heidi* was safe and familiar, as well as being culturally desirable; to the other, *Heidi* was, at best, irrelevant and at worst a symbol of adult oppression. And embarrassing.

To judge from the first list that we looked at, the criteria for nominating books as classics varies wildly. *To Kill a Mockingbird*, *Jane Eyre*, and *Oliver Twist* might be there because the narrators, at least initially, are children or teenagers; *Pride and Prejudice*, *Jane Eyre*, and *Wuthering Heights*, perhaps because (apart from being old) there is a certain teenage-girl passion about them; *Frankenstein* and *Tales of Mystery and Terror* may seem to speak to the teenage horror market; *The Count of Monte Cristo* and *The Hound of the Baskervilles* are among those many books that have slipped down the age ranges as being not quite suitable for adults anymore. (It is, not quite incidentally, instructive to see how successful reprints of old crime novels – 'classics' – have become the secret vice of certain readers.) In regards to *The Italian*, *Wives and Daughters*, and *The Woman in Black* – and from the second list, *Wise Children*, *Midnight's Children*, *To the Lighthouse*, and *Down There On a Visit* – I must leave it to my readers to speculate on the thinking behind their selection, or to imagine a childhood to which they might possibly appeal.

But many readers might insist there *must* be some qualitative element here. Not just any old book cannot become a classic, whatever the commercial pressures. As Winston Churchill remarked, history is written by the victors, and so the benchmarks for what we value culturally are set by those books that have survived. As the spate of revivals – notably in 'forgotten' women's writing, crime novels, and girls' school stories, among others – suggests, the writing of history that validates certain books as classics might have been very different. Arthur Ransome was only one of a legion of 'outdoor' writers of the 1930s, but because his books, by some quirk, survived, they *are* the standard. Whatever happened to M.E. Atkinson, Aubrey de Selincourt, David Severn, or Garry Hogg? Perhaps their 'classic' time will come.

Even if literary survival is largely a matter of luck, and the survivors set the standards for the others, surely there are 'landmark' books, which seem to have changed history, which *deserve* to be classics, and should be read in order for us (or the children) to understand literary history? This is a persuasive argument, but some of these books scarcely survive despite their 'historical importance': Captain Marryat's *Masterman Ready, or, the Wreck of the Pacific* (1841-2) was the beginning of the boys' sea story; Harriet Martineau's *The Crofton Boys* (1841), published sixteen years before *Tom Brown's Schooldays*, brought together all the essential features of the school story; and Joanna Cannan's *A Pony for Jean* (1937) marks the beginning of the pony story. These are significant books, but rarely read now.

Conversely, it doesn't much matter what a book is once it has joined the canon: students study *The Secret Garden* not because it is a particularly outstanding book of its period – or even an outstanding example of books of that period with the same plot – but because it has become a beacon to navigate by.

All of this might seem intriguing but irrelevant, were it not for the fact that the 'classics' regularly become a political tool. In 2011, Michael Gove, the then British Secretary of State for Education, began a campaign to get schoolchildren to read classic British literature, deriding the suggestion that 'the idea of a canon is outmoded'. In February 2016 the Department for Education, in association with Penguin, launched a 'new classic books in schools initiative.' The one hundred titles supplied cheaply to schools (in 'sets') are, according to the publicity,

2. What Makes a Children's Classic?

taken from Penguin's popular Black Classics series, range from the earliest writings to early 20th century works, span fiction and non-fiction, poetry and prose, and are intended to offer a springboard for children to discover the classics. All the titles are by authors who died before 1946 and are therefore out of copyright.

(This sounds like a familiar song – especially the final sentence.) There are only three recognisably 'children's' titles in the Penguin list – *Alice's Adventures in Wonderland*, *Treasure Island*, and *Little Women* – which raises intriguing questions about matching children's age and experience with the books they read. (Scholastic, not surprisingly has also launched a range of classics – and these *are* children's books.) What is revealing about the thinking behind these initiatives is that in terms of education *children's classics* don't count.

While the randomness of the process of becoming a classic, let alone the circularity by which those that survive determine the survival (or revival) chances of the rest, is clear, there often remains a stubborn resistance to it. Not *all* books can be equally good. Surely the books that feature in our third list – The Famous Five, Peter Rabbit, Biggles, Mary Lennox, Little Miss Bossy, and Alice – are not equally *valuable*.

There is an interesting paradox here. A traditionalist (and, as far as literary judgements are concerned, that means most of us) might argue that Peter Rabbit, Mary Lennox, and Alice have an obvious quality – after all, they feature in books that the literary culture agrees are important. On the other hand, the Famous Five, Biggles, and Little Miss Bossy are ephemeral and commercial, of no literary value. We are on dangerous ground if we try to impose an abstract 'literary' hierarchy on these books; perhaps it would be better to acknowledge that there is a distinction between books that *are* for children and which *were* for children. Those that become 'classic' because of age may have nothing to do with contemporary children or childhood.

If all this seems to lead deeper into mysterious areas of discussion, there are signs that the mystery is being solved. More and more it is being recognised (*pace* the politicians) that the most important, the most *classic* children's books are not those recognised as such by adults – but are those that are the true domain of childhood. These books are *not* accessible to adults and adult sensibilities and adult value-judgements. Enid Blyton claimed never to listen to any critic over the age of twelve, and as a classic writer for children, she is the genuine article.

3.

Why Were there no Nursery Rhymes before 1744?
Tom Thumb's Pretty Song Book, Vol. II

It is, of course, a trick question. Some nursery rhymes had been known and loved for many years before 1744. The question more properly put is, Why were there no substantial collections of nursery rhymes *published* before 1744?

Nursery rhymes, often in the form of short songs, have often been used by parents, perhaps at bedtime, to amuse or soothe their children. They seem to have come from all kinds of sources, such as adult folk songs, counting games, and even political squibs, and were widely known throughout Europe. There are references to them by the Roman poet Horace, and there may even be an echo of them in St Luke's Gospel (7.32) where Christ describes children shouting at each other in the marketplace:

> We piped for you and you would not dance.
> We wept for you, and you would not mourn.

They often derive from country folklore, and a French version of 'Thirty Days Hath September' appeared in the thirteenth century. Iona and Peter Opie, in their great work, *The Oxford Dictionary of Nursery Rhymes*, says that nearly 50 per cent of such rhymes are more than 200 years old, and that 12 per cent were known before 1649.

Some scholars have claimed that they all derive from some common European, or even Teutonic, source. There are certainly a number of English rhymes that seem to have equivalents in other languages, such as a Saxon version of 'Humpty Dumpty' and French and Spanish versions

3. Why Were there no Nursery Rhymes before 1744?

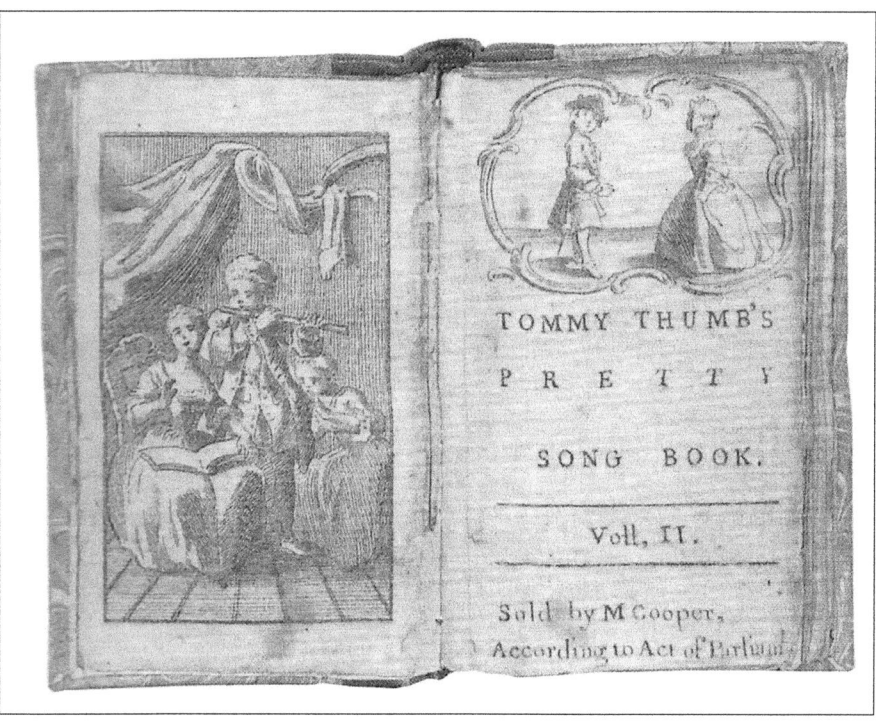

Half of a miniature masterpiece:
Mary Cooper's *Tommy Thumb's Pretty Song Book, Volume II* (1744).

of 'London Bridge'. But the possibility of translation from one country to another seems to be the most likely explanation. Danish children have their version of 'Jack and Jill':

> Jack og Jill
> Vent op de hill
> Og Jill kom tombling efter.

But this is not because of some common European version of the rhyme, but because British soldiers occupied parts of Denmark during the Napoleonic wars.

Although some of these rhymes occasionally appeared scattered in print in various publications before the eighteenth century – 'A Was an Apple Pie' appeared in 1671, for example – the question remains, Why was no substantial collection published before 1744?

This is largely because very few books were published for children before the seventeenth century on any subject. This is partly because of the cost of printing and the low levels of literacy that existed then, but also because of earlier attitudes towards children and their education. As printing became easier, more books became available for children in the seventeenth century. But seventeenth-century children's books tended to be either grammars or primers or religious works, such as James Janeways's *Token for Children* (1671-1772). Booksellers tried to make such books more attractive by including illustrations, and at the beginning of eighteenth-century editions of Aesop's *Fables* contained many pictures of animals. Such moral fables could help educate children, it was believed. Indeed, the great philosopher John Locke (1632-1704) in his *Thoughts Concerning Education* (1693) had argued that, in order to encourage reading, the child should be given 'some easy pleasant Book suited to his Capacity, wherein the entertainment that he finds might draw him on'.

Quite soon after this, books began to appear devised to make reading more attractive to children, such as T.W.'s *Little Book for Little Children* (*circa*. 1702), which actually included, among its exercises, the nursery rhymes 'A Was an Archer' and 'I Saw a Peacock with a Fiery Tail'. A trickle of more engaging books for children gradually followed, including John Gay's illustrated version of his *Fables* in 1727, the translation of Perrault's fairy tales into English in 1729, and Thomas Boreman's *Gigantic Histories* (1740), a whimsical account of giants and other curiosities.

The stage was being set then, you might say, for the appearance of *Tom Thumb's Pretty Song Book*, sold in two volumes by M. Cooper in 1744. This is a very remarkable work, a miniature book, measuring only 3x1¾ inches. It contained numerous illustrations, engraved on copper plates, and sold for sixpence. Although no copy of Volume I has actually survived, Volume II is extraordinary enough. Its sixty-four pages printed alternately in red and black, contains forty rhymes, including 'Sing a Song of Sixpence', 'Hickere, Dickere Dock [*sic*]', and 'Who Did Kill Cock Robbin [*sic*]'. But here for the very first time also appear such later favourites as 'Bah, Bah a Black Sheep', 'Lady Bird, Lady Bird', and 'Little Tom Tucker'. It is a little miracle.

The missing Volume I has never been found, nor much discovered about the role of the mysterious M. Cooper of the title page. Mary Cooper was a well-known London printer and publisher, but what part she played in compiling the collection remains a matter of conjecture. From various scattered pieces of evidence, however, Andrea Immel and Brian Alderson, two leading scholars in the history of children's literature, have tried to reconstruct what the missing Volume I might have contained. They suggest thirty-two other nursery rhymes including 'Baby Bunting', 'Cock a Doodle Do, My Dame Has Lost her Shoe', and 'See Saw Margery Daw', among other well-known rhymes.

In America, nursery rhymes are better known as 'Mother Goose Rhymes', a phrase that seems to have come from seventeenth-century France. When Charles Perrault's *Histoires, ou Contes du Temps Passé* was first published in France in 1697, its frontispiece was a picture of an old woman telling stories to three children. A plaque on the wall behind her read: *Contes de Ma Mére L'Oye* (Tales of Mother Goose). Later in the eighteenth century, a book called *Mother Goose's Melody* containing many nursery rhymes was published by John Newbery or one of his successors, and thus the name Mother Goose seems to have become associated with nursery rhymes.

Isaiah Thomas (1750-1831), a Bostonian publisher, produced *Mother Goose's Melody* around 1785, reproducing the earlier British work with few changes. This became very popular and led to many other versions, such as *Mother Goose's Quarto*, published by Munroe and Francis of Boston around 1825. In fact, there grew up a legend to the effect that *Mother Goose's Melody*, containing many American rhymes, was first published there long before Newbery's work appeared in Britain. According to this story, a certain Elizabeth Goose, who was born in 1665, had a daughter Elizabeth who was married to a printer, Thomas Fleet, and he published *Songs for the Nursery, or Mother Goose's Melodies* for children in America in 1719. No copy of this book has ever been found, and the story seems to have been largely made up by John Fleet Eliot, Thomas Fleet's grandson, in 1860.

In their outstanding collection, *The Oxford Dictionary of Nursery Rhymes*, Iona and Peter Opie discuss various attempts that have been made over the years to interpret the rhymes and invest them with political or symbolic significance. James Orchard Halliwell (1820-89), one of the earliest collectors, suggested, for example, that the famous characters Lucy Lockett and Kitty Fisher could be identified with two Caroline courtesans. It certainly looks as if 'the brave old Duke of York', who marched his men up and down hills, was based upon George III's son, Frederick, who was Commander-in-Chief of the British army and fought an unsuccessful campaign during the Napoleonic wars. But many of these attempted interpretations seem

The beginnings of popular culture in print:
a chapbook from c. 1700.

3. Why Were there no Nursery Rhymes before 1744?

too far-fetched to be credible. Was Bo-peep really based upon Mary Queen of Scots and Tommy Tucker on Cardinal Wolsey? Philip Larkin's friend Norman Iles produced one of the most recent examples of this kind of interpretation in his *Who Really Killed Cock Robin? Nursery Rhymes and Carols Restored to their Original Meanings* (Robert Hale, 1986). But the Opies will have none of this: 'The bulk of these speculations are worthless', they say, and it is hard to disagree.

After all, who can explain the magic of this verse first recorded in 1750?

> Hey diddle diddle,
> The cat and the fiddle,
> The cow jumped over the moon;
> The little dog laughed
> To see such sport,
> And the dish ran away with the spoon.

4.
Who Wrote Little Goody Two-Shoes?
Little Goody Two-Shoes (1765)

Today *Little Goody Two-Shoes* is almost forgotten. If it is remembered at all, it is as the subject of Christmas pantomimes, like *Dick Whittington* or *Jack and the Beanstalk*, or as some kind of half-digested phrase meaning something like 'a pious prig'. It is, in fact, the title of a children's book first published by the legendary bookseller John Newbery around 1765. It was a great success and frequently reprinted, sometimes as a chapbook, and was very popular in America. It seems to have been turned into stage-pantomime early in the nineteenth century, and continued to have been produced in London theatres and elsewhere almost to the present day.

The reason for its immediate success in the second half of the eighteenth century is not too difficult to determine, since, as well as telling a modest tale, it also reflected, in a straight-forward narrative form, some of the ideas and values that became dominant in that period.

The story itself is relatively simple. It is about a young girl called Margery Meanwell, and it begins when her father is driven off his farm by the landowner, Sir Timothy Gripe. Margery's parents die soon afterwards, leaving Margery and her brother, Tommy, to fend for themselves. They are befriended by Mr Smith, a kind clergyman, and also a charitable relative, who arranges for Tommy to go to sea and buys Margery a new pair of shoes. She is so proud of them that she acquires the name of Goody Two-Shoes.

But while living with Mr Smith, Margery has taught herself to read, and she now goes round the village teaching the other children the alphabet. She becomes a teacher, and is eventually asked to run the village school, or 'the A.B.C. College', as she calls it. Now elevated to the status of Mistress

4. Who Wrote Little Goody Two-Shoes?

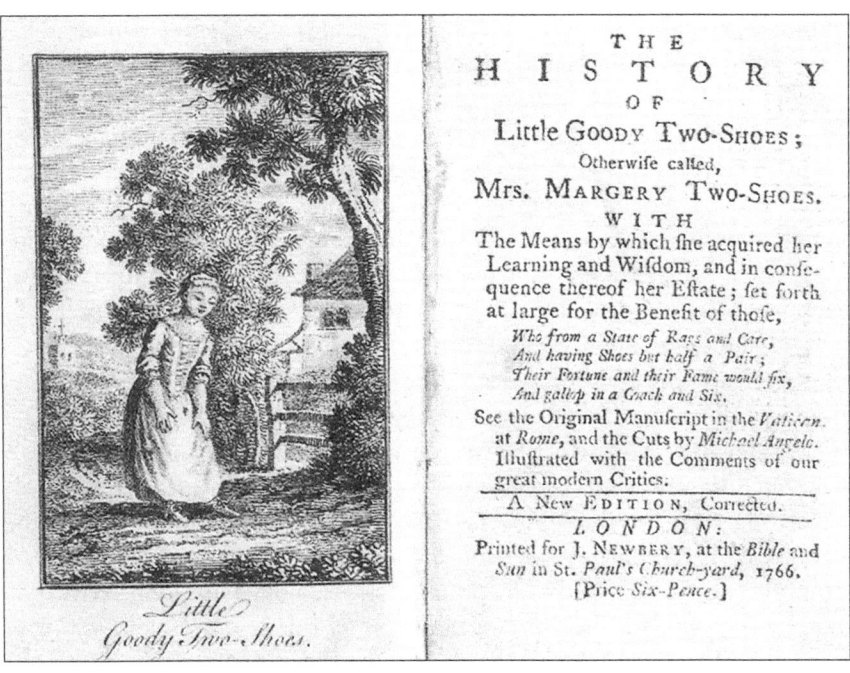

A mysterious best-seller from the master children's book publisher, John Newbery: *The History of Little Goody Two-Shoes* (1766).

Margery, she runs the school in humane and Christian ways. She stops boys being cruel to animals and acquires a number of pets, including a lamb and a pretty dog. As well as teaching the children, Margery also teaches the farmers' servants and other adults. She is called upon to settle their quarrels, and gradually becomes a great force for good in the village. Because she is wise and exercises reason in everyday life, she is accused of witchcraft, but the local justices dismiss the accusation.

Sir Charles Jones, a rich gentleman, admires her so much that he proposes to her, but Margery refuses to accept him until he has made proper provisions for his daughter. Their wedding day is made even happier when Margery's brother dramatically returns home from sea, now a rich gentleman himself. The story ends with Margery, who has now become Lady Jones, using her wealth to help the poor villagers and anyone in distress.

Illustrated by woodcuts, the book makes a modest attempt to teach reading by reproducing the letters of the alphabet in both upper and lower case, and by explaining syllables and sentences. But it is clear that the book owes its success to its simple rags-to-riches story, which embodies the Protestant work ethic. If you work hard and trust in God, as Margery does, though evils may come, righteousness will prevail and you will prosper.

No author's name is given on the title page of this once-popular story, however, and the question arises, 'Who wrote *Little Goody Two-Shoes?*'

John Nichols in his *Literary Anecdotes of the Eighteenth Century* (1812-15) claims that it was written by two brothers, Griffith and Giles Jones, although he offers no evidence for his assertion. (This idea might have been suggested by Margery's marriage to Sir Charles Jones.) Nearer to home, in 1794, Giles Jones's son Stephen had also claimed in his *New Biographical Dictionary* that the Jones brothers, along with John Newbery, were responsible for the stories *Goody Two-Shoes* and *Giles Gingerbread*.

Another claim for the authorship is made for the famous dramatist, novelist, and poet Oliver Goldsmith (1730?-74). Goldsmith is known to have worked for John Newbery from 1760 to 1764, around the time when *Goody Two-Shoes* was probably being written. We also know that Newbery helped to publish Goldsmith's *The Citizen of the World* in 1762, and he may also have had a hand in helping his nephew Francis Newbery to publish Goldsmith's novel, *The Vicar of Wakefield*, in 1766.

Many readers have pointed to certain similarities between Goldsmith's works and *Goody Two-Shoes*. The most striking example, perhaps, is the way in which, in the introduction to *Goody Two-Shoes*, its unnamed author describes the poor in the parish of Mouldwell and the way they have been ill-treated by the tenant farmers and the rich landowners. As a result, Margery and her family are thrown on the parish. Charlotte Yonge (1823-1901) was among a number of readers who saw parallels here with Goldsmith's picture of rural poverty in his poem 'The Deserted Village':

> Ill fares the land, to hastening ills a prey,
> Where wealth accumulates and men decay.

Readers have also found instances of humour and of pathos in the story that reminds them of Goldsmith's novel, *The Vicar of Wakefield*. Both Washington Irving (1783-1859) and William Godwin (1756-1836) supported the view that Goldsmith wrote *Goody Two-Shoes*.

4. Who Wrote Little Goody Two-Shoes?

But are these suggested similarities strong enough to confirm Goldsmith's authorship? If Goldsmith did have a hand in *Goody Two-Shoes,* it is very odd that Charles Welsh, the Victorian scholar, in his study of John Newbery entitled *A Bookseller of the Last Century,* lists numerous financial transactions between Goldsmith and Newbery, but found no record of any payment for *Goody Two-Shoes.* So we may say that the case for Goldsmith is not yet proven.

Matthew Grenby, in his introduction to the most recent edition of *Goody Two-Shoes* (Palgrave Macmillan, 2013), suggests that *Goody* may have been the combined work of several different authors. He points to the way in which book's 'editor' deliberately raises the idea that the book's preface and narrative were written by different people, and that Part Two of the story, the history of Margery's brother was only added later and seems almost tacked on.

Apart from looking for parallels in 'The Deserted Village' and *The Vicar of Wakefield,* however, one parallel to *Goody Two-Shoes* seems obvious. It is that of John Newbery's *A Little Pretty Pocket-Book* of 1744. The *Pretty Pocket-Book* is famous, of course, not only because it was the first book for children published by John Newbery, but because it was also one of the very first books – if not *the* first book – to be published for the amusement of children. (Earlier books had been works of education, instruction, morality, or religion.)

Yet the *Pretty Pocket-Book* is similar to *Goody Two-Shoes* in many ways. Both books contain a frontispiece, an introduction by the author, and numerous woodcuts. Unsurprisingly, because it is about the education and career of a teacher, *Goody Two-Shoes* has much to say about the teaching of the alphabet, syllables and sentences. But, perhaps more surprisingly, the chief entertainment of the *Pocket-Book* also consists of a series of illustrations to the letters of the alphabet, both upper and lower case, from its beginning with the grand 'A Play' to the final 'little z'.

Most importantly, *Little Goody Two-Shoes* is, as we have seen, an example of the Protestant work ethic. Margery is orphaned and poor, but borrows children's books to educate herself, and becomes a teacher, and eventually a very rich woman. The author of the work constantly attacks superstition, principally by criticising the cruel treatment of supposed witches, and endorses hard work and the use of reason. Margery's Christian lessons for the Conduct of Life include such rules as 'Industry is Fortune's right hand, and Frugality her left' and 'Make much of Three-pence, or you ne'er will be worth a Groat'.

Indeed the gloss on the book's title says the story reveals 'The means by which she [Margery] acquired her Learning and Wisdom, and in consequence thereof her Estate.'

Despite its little poems about children's games, and despite its charming woodcuts, *A Pretty Little Pocket-Book* preaches similar values to those of *Goody Two-Shoes*. Preceding the poems and the woodcuts, appears a letter addressed to the child readers' parents, guardians and nurses, which contains the following advice:

> Would you have a Wise Son, teach him to reason early. Let him read, and make him understand what he reads. No sentence should be passed over without a strict Examination of the Truth of it; and though this may be thought hard at first, and seem to retard the Boy in his Progress, yet a little Practice will make it familiar, and a Method of Reasoning will be acquired, which will be of Use to him all his Life after.

It is not surprising after this, to discover that most of the little verses accompanying the illustrations of children's games in the *Pretty Pocket-Book* also contain similar moral tags. Thus, the moral to the game of Chuck-Farthing tells us:

> *Chuck-Farthing*, like Trade,
> Requires great Care;
> The more you observe,
> The better you fare.

Isn't this similar to what *Little Goody Two-Shoes* advocates? One might almost say that *Goody Two-Shoes* is the fictional enactment of the principles lying behind *A Little Pretty Pocket-Book*. Is it not possible that they are by the same authors? But that only leads to another question, 'Who wrote the apparently anonymous *Little Pretty Pocket-Book*?'

5.

What (and Where) Are the Secret, Lost Books of Childhood – and Why Do they Matter?

The question that children's literature people – critics, teachers, bibliophiles – are most often asked (after 'What would be a suitable book for my five-year-old?') is – 'Do you know a book with a blue cover, about a little girl and a giraffe, which I read when I was little?', or something similar.

We do our (almost always unsuccessful) best – there are, after all, professional book-searchers whose livelihood depends on tracking such items – and the question is usually taken, both by the asker and the askee, to be just a matter of harmless whimsy. But it is often heartfelt whimsy; even those adults (and there are many) who are ruthless about keeping their childhood at a distance, seem to see these lost books as a secret, integral part of their lives. They are lodged somewhere in the brain, whether we like it or not.

And so each so-easily-dismissed mystery is actually disguising an astonishingly unaddressed cultural phenomenon. Most people, and almost all educationalists, would agree that what we read (or have read to us) as children is of massive and lasting importance; and yet very often the most important things that *are* read by or to us *are completely lost.* And not just to us, but to the world in general.

Consider this paradox. The output of children's books in Britain has been phenomenal: in 1939, 1,303 new titles were published; in 2015, some estimates make that over 10,000; backlists have been radically shorn, but estimates of 35,000 titles in print are not far to seek. In 2016, *The Bookseller* reported that

> The children's book market has grown 3.2% in 2015, thanks to gains in picture books, fiction and colouring-in titles. . . . According to data from Nielsen BookScan, the UK children's book market totalled £206m for the year to date (4th January – 12th September), up £6.37m for the same period in 2014. '2014 was an amazingly successful year for Children's with an 8.9% increase on 2013, but so far 2015 has been good too and continued the upwards trend.'

Three years later, although things were slowing, the numbers were still impressive:

> While the Children's market as a whole has plateaued in value since leaping 7% in 2016, with the full-year for 2017 posting a razor-thin 0.07% in growth, the Children's Non-Fiction category is booming in 2018 . . . [having] sold 3.75 million books for £24.7m for 2018 to date (up to 18th August), an 8.5% boost in volume and a 10.2% jump in volume on the same period in 2017.

A minuscule number of those books – both fiction and non-fiction – are reviewed, and an almost invisible fraction make it into the bookshops, let alone into the prized premium positions. The proportion that achieves any lasting fame or is canonised in the histories is even smaller. But they all sell *some* copies, and they all contact *some* children's minds, *somewhere*.

And then they disappear. It has often been observed (by frustrated bibliophiles, especially) that the most popular children's books – the most re-read, the most loved – are literally read to pieces. As we have seen, there are *no* surviving copies of the earliest books of Nursery Rhymes. Of course, some books that are read to destruction are easily replaced – the Blytons and Dahls and Rowlings of this world . . . but what of the rest? What of the non-bestsellers, the ones that we privately loved, and which have disappeared into attics, or have been ruthlessly cleared out to charity shops (often by unfeeling, downsizing parents)?

It is worth digging in this field for two reasons: the first is the personal satisfaction (or possibly trauma) to be derived from finding the books again; and the second is that to write the history of children's literature in terms of the survivors, the landmarks, the classics, is to seriously distort and simplify the way in which our culture works. Despite what we may have been taught about the hierarchy of literature and the universality of literary

5. What (and Where) Are the Secret, Lost Books of Childhood?

The stuff of personal nightmares:
Betty Larom's *The Story of Baba* (1949).

values, personal opinions *do* count. When we are dealing with these lost-but-not-forgotten books, we are in the world of visceral literary criticism. These books change lives. Individualism does matter!

This is such a personal matter that the only way of exploring it is personally – and we could almost, *Tristram Shandy*-like, leave a couple of blank pages here for you to fill in, to explore your own experiences. But while you are thinking about it, here are two personal examples – and how could they be anything but personal?

A few years ago, when we were clearing the attic of my late mother's house, I came across a beaten-up and slightly mouldy-smelling, old cardboard box containing some ancient toys and half a dozen books that I had as a child, which I had not seen or thought about (I thought) for maybe fifty years.

There was *The Golden Encyclopedia* 'with 1,500 items in full colour by Cornelius de Witt' – which probably has influenced what I think all encyclopedias should look like; *The 'Come On Steve' Annual* – apparently from a *Daily Express* cartoon strip; and the third was a happy book – happy in its associations, and cheerful reading even today. And a small, red hardback with a picture of a little boy, in a Christopher Robin smock, looking over the wall: *Timmy Turnpenny*. Let me give you a flavour:

> One day a little boy got lost.
>   He sat down on the pavement and began to cry. Along came the milkman, pushing his barrow.
>   'Milko, milko!' he cried.
>   He saw the little boy. He stopped his barrow.
>   'Hullo, sonny! What's the matter?'
>   'I'm lost. Boo-hoo!'
>   'Lost, are you? Well, let's see if we can find you. What's your name?'
>   'Timmy.'
>   'Timmy what?'
>   'Timmy nuffin.'
>   'Timmy Nuffin! That's a funny name. I never heard of a boy called Timmy Nuffin before.'
>   'I'm not Timmy Nuffin. I'm Timmy nuffin' else.'
>   'Oh, I see. But what's your Dad's name?'
>   'Daddy.'

. . . and so on. (I am glad to say that my daughters and my students also found that funny.)

Of course, I can merely cherish it, but as I am lucky enough to have the book in my hand – what is there to know about it? Why did it disappear? I can hardly have been the lone reader. As it turns out, I was far from being alone. On the verso of the title page – rather unusually, but fortunately for our current purposes, is the publishing history – 'First published April

5. What (and Where) Are the Secret, Lost Books of Childhood? 27

The ultimate wartime fantasy?
Small elephant captures large dictator, in Katharine Tozer's
Mumfie Marches On (1942).

1937... Reprinted May 1938; December 1941; November 1947'. So this unknown book was sufficiently popular to warrant the publisher, Harrap, to use some of its quota for paper (wartime restrictions were imposed in 1941 and lifted in 1949). Not an inconsiderable book, then, but invisible to the literary historians.

Before we arrive at the title page, there is a list of other books in this series called 'The Milly-Molly-Mandy Books', and they are each ninety-six pages. The list is partial, as some numbers are missing, and *Timmy Turnpenny* is number twenty. So I discovered that Joyce Lankester Brisley's *Milly-Molly-Mandy* – a book still in print, and in all the children's literature reference books – was, or became, the flagship of a series – and was presumably written to a 96-page formula (none of the reference books mention this). Only three of the series are actually about Milly-Molly-Mandy, but if *Timmy Turnpenny* is anything to go by, they might all occupy the lost world of the suburban and rural interwar years. Lucy Mangan, the *Guardian* columnist, sums up the nostalgia that many of us may feel for a period when we weren't even alive – that Arcadia, always just back over the hill. She liked Milly-Molly-Mandy as a child, but there was a problem:

> she was a torment because even then I knew the world in which these tiny, domestic non-adventures were set had already vanished. I would never live there, never buy a skein of wool for sixpence or wait for potatoes to bake in the village bonfire on Guy Fawkes night. It all seemed deeply unfair.

For a social historian in search of the true spirit of the age, this could be a starting point. Whatever happened to other books on the list – *The Story of Wimpy a Wump*, *Anders and Marta* (which turns out to be by Ursula Moray Williams), or *Bunchy*, another (and unsung) Joyce Lankester Brisley creation?

But back to *Timmy Turnpenny*. On the title page – and, significantly (because this is clearly a series format) not on the cover – we are told that the author is Rosalind Vallance, and the illustrator Joyce A. Johnson. Neither of these appear in any of the major reference books on children's literature or 20th Century Book Illustration. But a little research shows that Rosalind Vallance wrote or edited more than thirty books: collections of classic poems, anthologies, two volumes on Dickens for The Folio Society, and at least four other Timmy Turnpenny books. One of these, *Timmy and Jane*, is in the same series as *Timmy Turnpenny*. The illustrator of *Timmy Turnpenny*, Joyce A. Johnson, also illustrated some Enid Blyton books, including *A Queer Adventure*, which (perhaps not surprisingly) may be the only Blyton to appear under four titles. Joyce Johnson's illustrations also appeared in a reprint with another title, *The Marvellous Adventure* (it later appeared as *The Yellow Fairy Book* and *The Faraway Tree Adventure*).

With the benefit of the internet, it is much easier to trace books than it used to be; indeed, to enter the vast virtual warehouse where, as it were, the soul of the nation resides in its obscure children's books. But it is also quite easy to look in the wrong direction.

For example, another fondly remembered book of mine was Katharine Tozer's *Mumfie Marches On*, with its pale blue BOOK PRODUCTION WAR ECONOMY STANDARD cover. I can't imagine what I made of it at the time

5. What (and Where) Are the Secret, Lost Books of Childhood? 29

Once he cleaned all the shoes with Daddy's hairbrush

The ever-helpful child:
Joyce A. Johnson's illustration for Rosalind Vallance's *Timmy Turnpenny* (1937).

(indeed, I'm not sure what I make of it *now*) given that Mumfie, a small elephant who is in the Home Guard, manages with his friends to catch both Mussolini (masquerading as an ice-cream man) and Hitler:

> The silence was shattered by a series of guttural cries, rising to shrieks as the Leader of all the Germans danced madly in the road, clawing at the sharp end of his nose which was caught firmly in the vice-like grip of the rat-trap.
> The Führer danced and shouted . . .
> 'Shut up,' said Jelly. 'We're not the Reichstag. . . . Mumfie can ring through to the P.M. and get him fetched away.'

I could see why it was a forgotten book, and I had assumed that Mumfie had also vanished without trace – but not so. It seems he starred in a TV series between 1995-6, with a Carousel Books series, then two new series in 1994, and was in a feature-length film in 2014 from the Thomas the Tank Engine production stable.

If this research seems rather academic and high-minded when looking into a mouldy box, here is something more visceral. There was a fifth book in the box – one which I took out with some trepidation. It was a book that would be very far to seek, down among the literary detritus of the 1940s: *The Story of Baba* by Betty Larom (1949). Larom wrote at least one other book, *Happy's Holiday* (1964), and *Baba* (not to be confused with Babar) was published by Juvenile Productions, which seems to have been a resolutely downmarket, although quite long-lived, publisher of 'rewards'. It even had at least one Enid Blyton title (*Rumble and Tuff*) on its list. But all of that is irrelevant: for me, *The Story of Baba* was, and is, the stuff of nightmares. It promptly went back into the attic, and I forgot about it, until a couple of years ago when I was walking through a wood – no undergrowth, tall thin bare trunks – and I spent the rest of the day feeling uneasy, until I remembered. It was the very wood through which Baba the lost lamb was stalked by a fox – the sort of image that, when you are a child, you look at through protective fingers. Betty Larom may be forgotten (by the publishing world) but *The Story of Baba* is still lodged in my head, like it or (as it happens) not.

Those lost books, those unimportant, personal books are what one's intimate, private, reading-culture are really made of, and in their subtle ways, as a kind of literary mulch, they contribute to and perhaps ultimately determine the course of cultural history.

6.

The Curious History of Three Bears ... and a Lamb

'Goldilocks and the Three Bears' and 'Mary Had a Little Lamb'

At first sight 'The Story of the Three Bears' looks like that rare item – a successful modern literary fairy tale – for the poet-laureate Robert Southey (1774-1843) included it in a volume of his miscellaneous works, which were first published in 1839. Although Southey portrayed the intruder into the bears' house as a little old woman, rather than a young girl, the story rapidly became very popular and this was generally attributed to Southey.

But Southey had always said that he heard the story from his uncle William Tyler, and so the story must have been in some kind of circulation prior to 1839. In 1894, in fact, Joseph Jacobs (1854-1916), the great collector of English fairy tales, published a new selection, *More English Fairy Tales,* following his first selection of *English Fairy Tales* in 1890. *More English Fairy Tales* contains a story entitled 'Scrapefoot', about three bears who live in a castle that is visited by Scrapefoot, a fox. Scrapefoot has the impertinence to sit in the bears' chairs, drink their milk, and lie in their beds, and when the bears discover him, they throw him out of the window, and he gallops off never to visit the castle again.

Jacobs said that he acquired the tale from his friend, the illustrator, J.D. Batten (1860-1932), who said that he obtained it 'from Mrs H. who heard it from her mother over forty years ago'. It begins to look as if Southey's story had emerged from the common stock of many such traditional tales.

Then in 1951 a manuscript in the form of a home-made booklet entitled 'The Story of the Three Bears' was found in the Osborne Collection of Children's Books in Toronto, Canada. It appears that Eleanor Mure wrote the story, related in verse-form and illustrated by drawings, as a birthday present for her young nephew, Horace Broke. This version is dated 1831, six years before Southey's version appeared. In Mure's version the intruder is an old woman, and the bears drink milk, not porridge as in Southey's tale.

In other words, it looks as if 'The Story of the Three Bears' does come from the great tradition of folk tales after all. The three-fold repetition of the bears' complaints – 'Who's been eating my porridge? Who's been sitting in my chair? Who's been lying in my bed?' – is a regular feature of the folk tradition, found in such stories as 'The Three Little Pigs', for example. Other versions of the tale have now also been found in Germany and Norway. It was Joseph Cundall (1818-95), the great Victorian publisher of children's books, who first transformed the elderly female intruder into a young girl whom he called 'Silver Hair', in his *A Treasury of Pleasure Books for Young Children* in 1850, and the young heroine finally found her most popular identity as 'Goldilocks' in the *Old Nursery Stories and Rhymes*, illustrated by John Hassall and published *circa*. 1904.

The history of the nursery rhyme 'Mary had a Little Lamb' is almost as complicated as 'The Three Bears' and is even more controversial. The poem first appeared in print in America in September 1830 in the magazine the *Juvenile Miscellany* by Mrs Sarah Josepha Hale (1788-1879), a well-known writer and magazine editor, and it was reprinted later that year in *Poems for Our Children*, also by Mrs Hale.

But the poem has also been claimed quite vigorously by another American, Mary Sawyer (1806-1889), who was born in Sterling, Massachusetts. According to her account, Mary's father ran a farm that had a number of animals, including sheep. One wintry morning in March, when Mary was aged nine, she found in the sheep-pen a lamb that had been born the previous night but was so ailing that its mother had already abandoned it. Although the lamb was almost lifeless, Mary took it into the house where she fed and nursed it, and by loving care gradually brought it back to life. The lamb recovered its full strength, and came to possess a particularly fine white fleece. It became Mary's companion and friend, and did indeed follow her to school one day. There, for a lark, Mary decided to cover the lamb with a blanket and hide it under her seat in the classroom. But when she was called forward to recite, the lamb was disturbed and noisily clattered after her to the amusement of the teacher and the whole class.

It so happened that the school was being visited that day by a young student named John Roulstone, and he was so amused by the incident that he returned a few days later to give Mary a slip of paper containing the three verses:

6. The Curious History of Three Bears ... and a Lamb

> Mary had a little lamb,
> Its fleece was white as snow,
> And everywhere that Mary went,
> The lamb was sure to go.
>
> It followed her to school one day;
> Which was against the rule;
> It made the children laugh and play,
> To see a lamb at school.
>
> And so the teacher turned it out;
> But still it lingered near,
> And waited patiently about,
> Till Mary did appear.

The incident caused a great deal of amusement and gossip among Mary's friends and neighbours, as a result of which Mary made and sold stockings made from the lamb's wool for a local charity, carefully attaching to the stockings an autographed note to confirm their authenticity. Mary confirmed her account of the incident many times over the years, both to visitors and the local newspaper, although she always insisted that John Roulstone was the true author of the poem. The story was eventually taken up and promoted by the American millionaires, Mr Henry Ford and his wife, who published a pamphlet in 1928 entitled *The Story of Mary and her Little Lamb as Told by Mary and her Neighbors and Friends.* They supported Mary's version of the incident, and even paid for Mary's old Redstone Schoolhouse to be fully restored and moved for preservation from Sterling to Sudbury as a memorial.

But what are we to believe? Mrs Hale's claim has the advantage that the poem first appeared under her name in 1830, while Mary Sawyer's account seems to have appeared later. There is a family anecdote about the lamb in 1863, and at least one card attached to the sale of the wool seems to be dated 1880. John Roulstone died in 1822, so there is no way of obtaining further evidence from that source. Both ladies would seem to be unlikely liars. Yet Mrs Hale refuted Mary's claim in a letter written shortly before her death in 1879, while Mary was still alive; but Mary Sawyer (now Mrs Tyler) stuck to her story.

One possible explanation might be that, when John Roulstone heard of Mary's amusing little adventure, he recalled Mrs Hale's poem, and gave Mary its first three verses as an appropriate souvenir. But this seems unlikely, as the incident took place early in the nineteenth century, according to Mary Sawyer's own account, but Mrs Hale's poem did not appear until 1830.

Another explanation suggests that both women were right – or least not completely wrong. At the beginning of the nineteenth century, the Sawyer family lived in northern Massachusetts and the Hale family lived in the southern part of New Hampshire, both within the same general community, we might say. Here, we might conjecture that Mary Sawyer nursed her pet lamb, and John Roulstone produced the first three verses of the poem; and these got passed around, as an amusing anecdote and easy-to-remember poem, among family and friends, and then into the wider community of farmers, blacksmiths, carpenters, tradesmen of all sorts, rather like some urban myths today. Perhaps Sarah Hale, who was at the beginning of her literary career, recalled the amusing little rural incident with its verses, anonymous, as she thought, and turned them into a more literary poem about kindness to animals. The first three verses of the poem, we can see, relate the incident in the simplest language. But the last three verses contain not only dialogue, with questions, but point to an adult moral. The first three verses, we also notice, refer to the lamb only as 'it', while the last three verses describe it as a male. Is it possible that Sarah Hale added the last three verses to a poem that was already in the public domain?

> And then he ran to her, and laid
> His head upon her arm,
> As if he said, 'I'm not afraid,
> You'll keep me from all harm.'
>
> 'What makes the lamb love Mary so?'
> The eager children cry;
> 'Oh, Mary loves the lamb, you know,'
> The teacher did reply.
>
> 'And you, each gentle animal
> To you, for life, may bind,
> And make it follow at your call,
> If you are always kind.'

The truth is that we may never uncover the real history of what E.V. Lucas described as the best-known four-line verses in the English language.

7.

Charles Kingsley: Christian Socialist, Evangelical Storyteller, or Sexual Sadist?

The Water-Babies (1863)

If not one of the greatest, Charles Kingsley (1819-75) was certainly a very eminent Victorian. Born in a Devonshire village, the son of an Anglican clergyman, he studied first at King's College, London, and then at Magdalene College, Cambridge, where he obtained a second-class degree in Mathematics and a first in Classics. Partly through the influence of his fiancée, Kingsley entered the Church of England, and was ordained in 1842 and appointed a curate in the parish of Eversley in Hampshire. His first book, *The Saint's Tragedy*, a play in verse, was published in 1848.

During the bleak years of often violent unrest in England in the 1840s, Kingsley grew increasingly interested in social reform and became associated with F.D. Maurice (1805-72) and the Christian Socialist Movement. Under the name of 'Parson Lot', he began to write magazine articles and essays on social topics. His first two novels, *Yeast: A Problem* (1848) and *Alton Locke, Tailor and Poet* (1850), were passionately concerned with poverty and social problems. Kingsley was so opposed to the anti-social behaviour of the landowning classes that *Yeast* contains a socialist ballad about their evils:

> There's blood on your new foreign shrubs, squire;
> There's blood on your pointer's feet;
> There's blood on the game that you sell, squire,
> And there's blood on the game you eat!
>
> You have sold the labouring man, squire,
> Body and soul to shame,

> To pay for your seat in the House, squire,
> And to pay for the feed of your game.

But Kingsley was also seriously interested in natural history, especially marine life, and in 1855 published *Glaucus; or, the Wonders of the Shore*, where he wrote not only enthusiastically but knowledgeably about pink coralline, limpets, and starfish. He became a popular lecturer and well-known public figure. Appointed Chaplain-in-Ordinary to Queen Victoria in 1859, he was appointed Regius Professor of History at Cambridge in 1866, and tutor to the Prince of Wales a year later.

His adventure story *Westward Ho!* of 1855 had attracted many young readers, and in the same year Kingsley produced *The Heroes*, a retelling of Greek myths written for his own children. The story of how *The Water Babies* came about in 1862 was famously described by Kingsley's wife:

> Sitting at breakfast at the Rectory one spring morning this year, the father was reminded of an old promise, 'Rose, Maurice, and Mary have got their book [*The Heroes*], and baby must have his.' He made no answer, but got up at once and went into the study, locking the door. In half an hour he returned with the story of little Tom. This was the first chapter of *The Water-Babies*, written off without a correction.

The book, first serialised in *Macmillan's Magazine* from August 1862 till March 1863, and then published in book form in May 1863, was an immediate and lasting success. Within a year the first edition was sold out, and reprinting began. By the end of the nineteenth century it had become one of the most popular children's books ever published in Britain and has never been out of print.

Although *The Water-Babies* has a number of weaknesses, such as its over-didactic approach and numerous digressions, the reasons for the book's popularity are fairly obvious. Although it begins with an account of an abused chimney-sweep, as if it is to be a Christian Socialist novel about the condition of the working classes, it soon changes direction. It uses the device of a modern fairy tale or fantasy to describe the experiences of Tom, the boy chimney-sweep, in an extraordinary adventure. After his disastrous visit to Harthover Place and his fall down a chimney into a little girl's bedroom, Tom runs away and disappears into the river, where he has many adventures under water, and encounters all kinds of extraordinary characters until he reaches the Other-end-of-Nowhere. There he meets again his cruel master, the old chimney-sweep Mr Grimes, and is reunited with Ellie, the

7. Charles Kingsley

Erotic theology:
one of the sketches made by Charles Kingsley for his future wife, Fanny (1843).

little girl. But this narrative, it is clear, is a carefully worked out and at times a rather moving Christian allegory. At the beginning of the tale, young Tom is an unreformed rascal, full of pluck and spirit but completely amoral; and it is through his experiences in the water, a spiritually-cleansing process, particularly in his encounters with Mrs Bedonebyasyoudid and the old Irish woman, that he learns to cast aside greed and selfishness, and even to weep for and help his old cruel master.

All of this is told with a robust inventive energy and humour, even in the digressions about Darwinism, Natural History, or Medicine, so that the story seems to rush along. Although Kingsley's account of child labour in the opening chapters is what many readers tend to remember, it is really the book's vigorous, sometimes satirical, treatment of Victorian life, such as the attack on rote-learning, or the lyrical description of a dragonfly, that gives *The Water-Babies* its unique flavour.

However, one also has to recognise that Kingsley's book also contains some remarkably disturbing elements, which have aroused a good deal of criticism. The work is didactic, as were many children's books of the period. Many writers agreed with the proverbial saying: 'spare the rod and spoil the child', and believed that the chastisement of children was necessary in order to promote their virtue. (Lowood Asylum, a charitable institution in Charlotte Brontë's *Jane Eyre* of 1847, is a gruesome example of this.) And Kingsley is actually rather more amusing and tolerant than some of his predecessors, such as Mrs Mary Sherwood (1775-1851), author of the notoriously frightening *History of the Fairchild Family* (1818-47).

But Kingsley clearly intended his story to teach children how to behave. In particular, however, whenever he portrays Tom or other characters behaving badly, he also shows them being punished for their sins. Under water, Tom is clearly thoughtlessly cruel to many of the strange creatures he meets; for example, he torments anemones and crabs and trout. But then Mrs Bedonebyasyoudid appears, a tall lady with a great birch-rod under her arm, and she punishes Tom for his behaviour by putting a pebble in his mouth. When he helps himself to some of her lollipops, he discovers that he has become untouchable because he is covered all over with prickles. But it is not just Tom but wrong-doers of all kinds who are punished everywhere. Careless mothers are made to wear tight corsets and cruel doctors made to drink evil medicines. Rough schoolmasters have their heads thumped and callous nursery maids have pins stuck in them. It is not surprising that even Tom begins to think Mrs Bedonebyasyoudid a little spiteful, and the critics have agreed with him. One of them, novelist and Victorian scholar Gillian Avery, in her *Nineteenth Century Children*, calls Mrs Bedonebyasyoudid 'a stern figure of retribution'. She also says that in Kingsley's mind 'the idea of crime and punishment . . . recur with frightening regularity'.

Some critics have gone even further, and found the book sexually disturbing. Kingsley's obsession with water and washing was a lifelong characteristic, we know, even before he wrote *The Water-Babies*. If he found a spot on his clothes, he was conscious of it all day, he said, which seems to suggest some kind of guilt complex. The writer, Maureen Duffy, in *The Erotic World of Faery* (1972) even goes so far as to call *The Water-Babies* a fable about masturbation. Tom's plunge into the water is like a questing penis, she argues, and suggests that Tom is a little boy with dirty habits who must be purified before he is fit to enter heaven with Ellie. If you don't learn to leave sweets alone, you will grow prickles and be unlovable.

Humphrey Carpenter in his book *Secret Gardens* (1987) suggests that *The Water-Babies* is full of sexual symbolism, beginning with a chapter that suggests rape when it describes Tom working his way down a chimney into Ellie's white bedroom, which is in itself a symbol of virginity. As a writer, Carpenter argues, Kingsley was an entirely destructive critic of women and society, 'a sexual sadist (in imagination if not in fact)'. It is a formidable accusation.

Even if we think that the critics go too far, there is no doubt that reading Charles Kingsley's *The Water-Babies* can raise some awkward questions.

8.

Who Was the Real William Brighty Rands?
Lilliput Levee (1864)

The children's verse of the Victorian poet William Brighty Rands (1823-82) has not been without some recognition. F.J. Harvey Darton discusses his work in his classical account of *Children's Books in England* (1932, rev. ed. 1982); Iona and Peter Opie include eight of his poems in the *Oxford Book of Children's Verse* (1973); and Morag Styles quotes him in her study of children's poetry, *The Garden and the Street* (1998).

Even so, the work of the man whom the essayist and novelist James Payne called 'the laureate of the nursery' seems hardly known today. The last selection of his work, *Miss Hooper's Hoop and other Poems,* was published in 1949, and an attempt by his great-grandson to promote his ancestor's work by producing in 2005 an attractive CD entitled *Lilliput Lyrics* sold only a handful of copies.

One explanation for Rands's neglect surely lies in the confusion he created in the ways he deliberately mystified readers over the authorship of his publications, for this prolific author seemed to delight in producing his works under a variety of names or without any name at all. He wrote *Chaucer's England* (in two volumes) under the name of Matthew Browne in 1869; *The Shoemaker's Village,* a two-volume novel, under the name of Henry Holbeach in 1871; and his major children's books *Lilliput Levee* (1864) and *Lilliput Lectures* (1871) anonymously.

Why Rands was so reluctant to publish under his own name remains a mystery. One possibility is that he was so embarrassed by the poor quality of an early book of adult verse, a sub-Tennysonian volume entitled *The Chain of Lilies* (1857), that he resolved to conceal the source of his later

8. Who Was the Real William Brighty Rands?

THE PENANCE OF THE LITTLE MAID

I MET a fair maiden, I saw her plain,
   In the five-acre when the corn was mellow,
Counting her fingers again and again,
   Her kirtle was green, her hair was yellow.

The bucolic William Brighty Rands:
from an 1899 edition of *Lilliput Lyrics* illustrated by Charles Robinson.

works. The explanation that he himself offered was that, as he was employed full-time for most of his adult life, first as a foreign correspondent in a merchant's office and subsequently as a Parliamentary reporter, he needed to conceal his literary activities from his employers in order to protect his professional career.

However, the most likely explanation is that Rands was unwilling to reveal any information about his private life because it would have seemed so irregular in respectable Victorian England. Born the son of a small shopkeeper in Chelsea in 1823, Rands received only a limited formal education. But he was a precocious reader and, though he got his first job in a lawyer's office when he was only thirteen, he continued to educate himself, partly, it is said, from his voracious reading at second-hand bookstalls; and so he is believed to have taught himself Latin, Greek, French, Spanish, and German. Having also taught himself shorthand, he worked as a reporter in the House of Commons from 1857, and began contributing to numerous journals and magazines, including *The Contemporary Review, St. Paul's Magazine* and *Good Words for the Young,* publishing articles on George Eliot, George MacDonald, and Nathaniel Hawthorne, among others. In addition to the adult poems in *The Chain of Lilies,* Rands also published a Dickensian tale, *The Frost Upon the Pane* in 1854, his two-volume study of Chaucer in 1869, and his young children's books – *Lilliput Leveé* (1864, 1867), *Lilliput Lectures* (1871), and *Lilliput Legends* (1872). He was, you might say, a pretty successful Victorian all-round man of letters.

But although Rands married Mary Ditton, a cheese-maker's daughter, in 1846, and they had three children, he left her after twelve years of marriage to live with another woman, Hannah Rolls, by whom he had four more children, and whom he subsequently married after his first wife's death in 1881. Like his parents, Rands was a devout, if unorthodox Christian, and, though he continued to support his first family materially, there seems little doubt that he felt guilty about his private life and tried to keep it secret from the public. There are stories of Rands hustling the children of his second family into side streets in order to avoid passers-by. There was also a reluctance to receive visitors into the family home, except, it is said, for occasional callers who were surreptitiously given parcels of food and clothing that, it is thought, were to be delivered to Rands's first family.

Rands seems to have been a somewhat eccentric father. On the one hand, he made no arrangements for his children to be educated formally, but, although brusque at times, he encouraged them to read as freely and widely as possible, and he did not believe in corporal punishment. The children grew up to become very well informed, and this was probably because he disliked talking down to them. He believed in what he called 'a natural style of writing', and felt that 'the elements upon which all the great initial questions must be settled are apprehended by children as well as by grown-up people'. In order to do this he tried to find 'childlike ways of putting certain things'.

Altogether, Rands published in *Lilliput Levee* and *Lilliput Lectures* about 125 poems in book form, although his final output must be far greater than this because many more seem to have been published in magazines, sometimes anonymously, and have not yet been properly collected. But if their range and variety is impressive, the same kind of psychological difficulty that was apparent in his adoption of so many different pseudonyms also applies here in his children's poetry, for Rands uses a variety of genres and voices as if unsure of his literary identity.

Many are extravagantly comic in a fairly straightforward kind of way, rather in the manner of Edward Lear, such as 'The Duck and her Ducklings', 'Obstinate Cow', and 'There Was a Giant'. Other comic verse takes the form of cautionary tales, such as 'Miss Hooper's Hoop' and 'Godfrey Gordon Gustavus Gore', a poem about a little boy who persistently refuses to close doors behind him until his parents threaten to send him as a punishment to Singapore. These poems cannot help but remind the reader of Hilaire Belloc's *Cautionary Tales for Children* published much later in 1907.

Some of Rands's poems are religious, reminding us of his devout parents and non-conformist background. Of these the best known is 'The World', which begins with the line, much celebrated in its day – 'Great, wide, beautiful, wonderful World', found in the *Lilliput Lectures*. Other poems remind us of William Blake's *Song of Innocence and Experience* of 1794, such as 'The Flowers':

> When Love arose in heart and deed
> To wake the world to greater joy,
> 'What can she give me now!' said Greed,
> Who thought to win a costly toy.
>
> He rose, he ran, he stoop'd, he clutch'd;
> And soon the Flowers that Love let fall,
> In Greed's hot grasp were fray'd and smutch'd,
> And Greed said, 'Flowers! Can this be all?'
>
> He flung them down and went his way,
> He cared no jot for thyme or rose;
> But boys and girls came out to play,
> And some took these and some took those –

> Red, blue, and white, and green and gold;
> And at their touch the dew return'd,
> And all the bloom a thousand fold –
> So red, so ripe, the roses burn'd!

Perhaps the most distinctive of all Rands's poems, however, are those where he seems to enter into the child's feelings and imagination, almost inhabiting the child's voice. These are often simple poems, which surely anticipate Robert Louis Stevenson's *A Child's Garden of Verses* of 1885, such as 'The Pedlar's Caravan':

> I wish I lived in a caravan,
> With a horse to drive, like the Pedlar-man!
> Where he comes from nobody knows,
> Or where he comes from, but on he goes. . . .
>
> With the pedlar-man I should like to roam,
> And write a book when I come home;
> All the people would read my book,
> Just like the travels of Captain Cook.

Other poems are more fantastical, such as 'I saw a New World', where the poet wonders what the world would be like if everyone and everything were to be uniform and identical. In 'Lilliput Levee', Rands conjures up another fantastic universe where children take over the world and seize control of the adults:

> Oh, the Glorious Revolution!
> Oh, the Provisional Constitution!
> Now the Children, clever bold folk,
> Have turn'd the tables upon the Old Folk!
>
> They seiz'd the keys, they patrolled the street
> They drove the policeman off his beat,
> They built barricades, they stationed sentries –
> You must give the word, when you come to the entries!
>
> They dress'd themselves in the Riflemen's clothes,
> They had pea-shooters, they had arrows and bows,
> So as to put resistance down –
> Order reigns in Lilliput-town! . . .

8. Who Was the Real William Brighty Rands?

> They offered a prize for the laziest boy
> And one for the most Magnificent toy. . . .
>
> Lilliput-land was a paradise
> Of everything you can say that's nice!
> A magic lantern for all to see,
> Rabbits to keep and a Christmas tree.

There you have him. Matthew Browne? Henry Holbeach? Edward Lear? Hilaire Belloc? William Blake? And Robert Louis Stevenson? Will the real Brighty Rands please stand up?

9.

Why Are there so many Dead Parents in Children's Books?

Children's books are chillingly dangerous places in which to be a parent. Obviously, in fiction, children have to be given a space to play and a space to have adventures, and these spaces do not often involve parents – after all, children's books are there to give the illusion of freedom.

Sometimes, parents (the lucky ones who survive) or surrogate parents, act as guardians, just offstage. In Arthur Ransome's Swallows and Amazons series, Mrs Walker and Mrs Blackett are on the edge of the lake, in case of accidents, but survival is up to the children. As Commander Walker cheerfully observes, 'Better drowned than duffers. If not duffers, won't drown.' Enid Blyton's epic series, The Famous Five, begins with similarly detached parents, as their Daddy says about the family summer holidays,

> 'Mother and I won't be able to go with you this year. Has Mother told you?'
> 'Well, this time Daddy wants me to go to Scotland with him,' said Mother. 'All by ourselves! And as you are really getting big enough to look after yourselves now, we thought it would be rather fun for you to have a holiday on your own, too.'

(Incidentally, Julian is twelve, Dick and George are eleven, and Anne is ten.)

Sometimes the children are sent away to school – sometimes with fond farewells at the breakfast table or at stations, but more often not. In one notable and extreme case, Elinor M. Brent-Dyer's *The School at the Chalet* (1925), two orphaned girls, Madge and Joey, establish their own school. Sometimes the

9. Why Are there so many Dead Parents in Children's Books?

SHE LAID HER DOLL EMILY ACROSS HER KNEES, * * * * * AND SAT THERE, HER LITTLE BLACK HEAD RESTING ON THE BLACK CRAPE, NOT SAYING ONE WORD NOT MAKING ONE SOUND.

The archetypal orphan:
Sara and Emily in Frances Hodgson Burnett's fist version of
A Little Princess, Sara Crewe or What Happened at Miss Minchin's (1888)
illustrated by Reginald B. Birch.

children are evacuated to the countryside away from parents who are kind, for example with Nina Bawden's *Carrie's War*: ' "Oh, it'll be such fun," their mother had said when she kissed them goodbye at the station'; or who are homicidal, as in the case of Willie's mother in Michelle Magorian's *Goodnight Mr Tom*; or simply invisible, as in *The Lion, the Witch and the Wardrobe*.

Often, parents are simply irrelevant for the majority of the plot, as the children depart to parallel worlds (*Peter Pan* is probably the most obvious example), although in the case of Neil Gaiman's *Coraline*, the alternative world also contains alternative parents. Sometimes the alternative world is self-contained – there are no parents in *Winnie-the-Pooh*.

This has been a frighteningly common approach – frightening, perhaps to loving parents who give wholesome books to their children – that the parents are simply bumped off, and this is regardless of the age of the intended audience.

Thus one might innocently settle down to read the bright and jolly-looking *The Story of Babar, the Little Elephant* by Jean de Brunhoff, possibly lured by A.A. Milne's preface: 'If you love elephants you will love Babar and Celeste. If you have never loved elephants you will love them now. If you who are grown-up have never been fascinated by a picture-book before, then this is the one which will fascinate you.' Enthusiastic stuff, and things begin cheerfully enough: 'In the Great Forest a little elephant was born. His name was Babar. His mother loved him dearly and used to rock him to sleep with her trunk, singing to him softly the while.'

So far (page 3), so good. However, two openings later we find explicit pictures with this script: 'One day Babar was having a lovely ride on his mother's back when a cruel hunter, hiding behind a bush, shot at them. He killed Babar's mother. The monkeys hid themselves, the birds flew away, and Babar burst into tears. The hunter ran up to catch poor Babar.'

At least when Beatrix Potter kills off Peter Rabbit's father (on the second opening of *The Tale of Peter Rabbit*), she makes a joke about it:

> 'Now my dears,' said old Mrs Rabbit one morning, 'you may go into the fields or down the lane, but don't go into Mr McGregor's garden: your Father had an accident there; he was put in a pie by Mrs McGregor.'

It is striking that children in 1902 were (or were assumed to be) a lot tougher-minded than contemporary children. In some current editions, Mrs Rabbit's imprecation simply ends with 'don't go into Mr McGregor's garden', and in another she modifies the warning: 'He doesn't like rabbits. He will try to catch you.'

9. Why Are there so many Dead Parents in Children's Books?

At the beginning of the nineteenth century, the family unit was vitally important to culture and children's literature, but as the century wore on and life became more religiously uncertain, parental carnage in fiction sets in. Francis Hodgson Burnett was particularly savage. The death of Little Lord Fauntleroy's father is announced in line seven of Chapter One. In *A Little Princess*, Sara Crewe, whose mother had died when she was born (which happens disproportionately often in fiction), then loses her father in India. As the wicked Miss Minchin puts it, 'Captain Crewe is dead . . . . He has died without a penny. That spoiled, pampered, fanciful child is left a pauper on my hands.' A few years later, in *The Secret Garden*, Mary Lennox's father and mother (serve her right!) are carried off by the cholera, Colin's mother falls off a swing and dies in childbirth. Tom Sawyer and Dorothy Gale are orphans; the narrator of J. Meade Falkner's *Moonfleet* is casual enough about it all: 'I was fifteen years of age when this story begins. My father and mother had both been dead for years.'

In fact, orphans roamed, if not ruled, the world. We meet a five-year-old orphan on her way to live with her grandfather in *Heidis Lehr- und Wanderjahre*; we meet Anne Shirley, just arrived from an orphanage waiting for a new home on a Canadian railway station in *Anne of Green Gables*; and the determinedly cheerful Pollyanna is an orphan (named for her two aunts – all her other brothers and sisters had died too). Occasionally, parents are obliquely mourned, as in Nesbit's *The Treasure Seekers*. Oswald, the narrator, comes straight to the point: 'There are six of us besides Father. Our Mother is dead, and if you think we don't care because I don't tell you much about her, you only show that you do not understand people at all.'

Mostly, however, these deaths are matter-of-fact, as with Pippi Longstocking:

> Once upon a time Pippi did have a father whom she loved very much. And of course she once had a mother too, but that was so long ago that she couldn't remember her at all. Her mother died when Pippi was a tiny little baby, lying in her cot and crying so terribly that no one could stand to come near. Pippi thought her mother was now up in heaven, peering down at her daughter through a hole. . . . But Pippi had not forgotten her father. He was a sea captain and sailed the great seas, and Pippi sailed with him on his ship until one day a big storm blew him overboard and he disappeared.

At least the captain was remembered. Perhaps the peak of brutality was reached in Noel Streatfeild's generation with *The Circus is Coming* (1936), which begins briskly: 'Peter and Santa were orphans. When they were babies their father and mother were killed in a railway accident, so they came and lived with their aunt.'

As for the Fossil girls in *Ballet Shoes*, Pauline's parents died on the *Titanic*, Petrova's died in Russia, and Posy's mother abandoned her. Even Arthur Ransome killed off the Amazons' father. Parents, then, are disposable and (with a few exceptions, such as Nancy Blackett's brief displays of emotion in *Swallowdale*), generally not much missed. Tolly, in *The Children of Green Knowe*, thinks that 'he wished he had a family like other people – brothers and sisters, even if his father were away. His mother was dead. He had a stepmother, but he hardly knew her, and was miserably shy of her.' That was 1954, and thirty years later that shyness would have turned to dislike or fear.

Thus the idea of the absent parent as a plot device gradually developed through the nineteenth century. At first it gave the bereaved children a motive for piety; later – in that brief period of idealised childhood innocence, from about 1900 to 1930 – it reflected the idea of a protected play-space; and this was maintained, almost absent-mindedly, into the post-World War II era. But by the 1980s, as fantasy gave way to realism, it became almost mandatory to dispose of one or the other the parents to provide some sort of conflict, deprivation, or, as in the case of Anne Fine's *Crummy Mummy and Me*, a role reversal. In the world of Jacqueline Wilson's deceptively dark comedy, her sad and brave female heroes exist in dysfunctional families, although the world is a still a pretty dangerous place for fathers, who are inclined to disappear, one way or another. In Wilson's breakthrough novel, *The Story of Tracy Beaker* (1991), Tracy writes 'I don't have a dad', and that's about it.

In chapter two of *Harry Potter and the Philosopher's Stone*, we are told (possibly with a sly nod from the author towards traditions in fiction) that Harry's parents were killed in a car crash. In fact (spoiler alert!) they were killed while defending him from evil. As Dumbledore says, 'Your mother died to save you. If there is one thing that Voldemort cannot understand, it is love. . . . To have been loved so deeply, even though the person who loved is gone, will give us some protection for ever.'

Roald Dahl initially embraced the tradition with characteristic gusto: in his first children's book, *James and the Giant Peach*, James's parents are killed when a rhinoceros escapes from the zoo. In *The BFG*, Sophie is an orphan:

> 'I don't have a mother and father,' Sophie said. 'They both died when I was a baby.'
>
> 'Oh, you poor little scrumplet!' cried the BFG. 'Is you not missing them very badly?'
>
> 'Not really,' Sophie said, 'because I never knew them.'

However, Dahl could see the advantage of parents as foils – good in *Charlie and the Chocolate Factory* and despicable in *Matilda* ('Mr Wormwood was a small ratty-looking man whose front teeth stuck out underneath a thin ratty moustache').

In a strange way, recent children's fiction in general has reverted to the idea of the integrated family as an ideal, if not something based on reality – but the convention of disposing inconvenient adults is, as it were, far from dead. A trawl through the current publishers' catalogues – where there is dysfunction aplenty – produces examples such as Eric Lindstrom's *Not if I See You First* (2015) in which Parker, at age seven, is blinded in a car crash that kills her mother, and her father commits suicide (or possibly has a heart attack).

If that sounds like selective special pleading, it's worth noting that *all* of the past five Carnegie Medal Winners (for the best children's book of the year) have had some parental deaths – although that is perhaps not surprising, as they are an unremittingly miserable bunch. The female hero of *Buffalo Soldier* (2015), the story of the only black woman who served in the US army (as a man) in the nineteenth century, has a stepmother who is raped and hung. Then there is *Bunker Diary* (2014) (mother dead, father estranged), *Maggot Moon* (2013) (parents 'disappeared' in a totalitarian state), *Monsters of Men* (2012) (parents dead two books ago), and *The Graveyard Book* (2011) (family murdered). Merry stuff.

And down among the bestsellers, it is almost cheering to note that the parents of Alex Rider, Anthony Horowitz's astonishing (and deservedly successful) young spy hero, were splendidly traditional. Three pages into *Stormbreaker* (2000) we learn: 'He had never known his own parents. They had died in an accident, that one a plane crash, a few weeks after he had been born.'

The logic of authors is clear: if children/teenagers, are to be fully empowered, they need to move on from their parents, but the mystery remains, why does their shuffling off the stage have to so often be so brutally radical? It seems strange that child readers, in order to gain the freedom to play and explore and adventure, have to step over the corpses of those who would most want to protect them. It seems deeply Freudian. Does this represent a curious relationship between authors and their childhoods and their parents?

But if the mystery remains, the moral is clear. If you are a parent, steer clear of a part in a children's book.

10.

Was Lorna Doone really Married?

R.D. Blackmore, *Lorna Doone* (1869)

Lorna Doone, R.D. Blackmore's great historical romance about Exmoor has never quite disappeared from the public eye, unlike such similar Victorian works as Charles Reade's *The Cloister and the Hearth* (1861) or Charles Kingsley's *Westward Ho!* (1855), or *Hereward the Wake* (1866). Every so often it resurfaces, usually as a screen adaptation, having been filmed no fewer than ten times, most recently by BBC TV in 2001. There is something about the story that compels interest, despite its three-volumed length.

The appeal of the young heroine is partly responsible for this, for Lorna is surely the most attractive literary heroine since Sophia Western in Fielding's *Tom Jones* (1749). Here she is when the young John Ridd first sees her:

> I had never heard so sweet a sound as came from between her bright red lips, while there she knelt and gazed at me; neither had I ever seen anything so beautiful as the large dark eyes intent upon me, full of pity and wonder. And then, my nature being slow, and perhaps for that matter, heavy, I wandered with my hazy eyes down the black shower of her hair, as to my jaded gaze it seemed, and where it fell on the turf, among it (like an early star) was the first primrose of the season. And since that day, I think of her, through all the rough storms of my life, when I see an early primrose.

But there are many other elements in the story that contribute to its popularity. There is, first of all, its setting on Exmoor, a landscape of

10. Was Lorna Doone really Married?

Timeless romance, timeless landscape:
the Doone Valley, Exmoor, Devon.

farms and villages and running water, and the chequered fields with their red Devonian earth contrasting with the once-forested hills. There is the appeal of the rich variety of characters – not only John and Lorna, but Tom Faggus, the highwayman; Reuben Huckback, the shopkeeper; Jeremy Stickler, the King's Messenger; and an impressive array of women including John's widowed mother and his sisters, Annie and Lizzie; Mother Meldrum, the local witch; and Gwenny Carfax, the interfering maid. There is the wonderfully dramatic scene near the end of the novel when the heroine is shot in the parish church on her wedding day. At the heart of the whole story, of course, is the long-standing feud between the ruthless Doone clan of brigands and all the decent folk of Exmoor at a time in seventeenth-century England when law and order only operated sporadically, and the

Monmouth Rebellion of 1685 typified the threat of violent anarchy. John's bitter life-and-death struggle with Carver Doone, the murderer of his father, crystallises this conflict perfectly.

But this great historical romance is also a kind of *bildungsroman*, the autobiographical account of a young man's self-development and social success, as he struggles to win Lorna's love in a time of turbulence and political upheaval. The reader sees the hero advance from being plain John Ridd, the son of a yeoman, to becoming Sir John Ridd, a gentleman-farmer, married to a rich heiress. He is an almost perfect example of the Protestant work ethic, the ideology that had become so dominant in the Victorian age when Blackmore wrote his story.

But if John's struggles with Carver Doone epitomise the lawlessness of the period, his attempts to woo and win Lorna reveal the problems of the class system. John is a yeoman-farmer, like his father before him, and he is brave and loving and true, an accomplished lover in Lorna's eyes. But the Doones are a family of aristocrats and land-owners, and Lorna's rank, as the granddaughter of Sir Ensor Doone, makes John an unacceptable suitor. Lorna is 'born of the oldest families remaining in North Europe', Sir Ensor tells John. 'All marriage is a wretched farce, even when man and wife belong to the same rank of life. . . . But when they are not so matched, the farce would become a long dull tragedy, if any thing were worth lamenting.' The local wise woman, Mother Meldrum, also tries to warn John off the Doone family.

John Ridd himself has doubts as to whether he should marry someone from a higher social class. These doubts grow even more when it is discovered that Lorna is the rich daughter of the Earl of Dugal, and she becomes a member of the King's royal household and the Queen's attendant. Even Lorna's maid Gwenny Carfax hates the match and deliberately withholds Lorna's loving letters to John in the hope of destroying their relationship. 'Because 'ee be'est below her so,' she defiantly tells John. 'Her shanna' have a poor farmering chap, not even if he were a Carnishman. All her land, and all her birth – and who be you, I'd like to know.'

Fortunately Lorna's love and recognition of John's true worth is unswerving, as she eloquently tells him:

> In the first place, it is quite certain, that neither you nor I can be happy without the other. Then what stands between us? Worldly position, and nothing else. I have no more education than you have, John Ridd; nay, and not so much. My birth and ancestry are not one whit more pure than yours, although they may be better known. Your descent from ancient freeholders, for five-

10. Was Lorna Doone really Married?

and-twenty generations of good, honest men, although you bear no coat of arms, is better than the lineage of nine proud English noblemen out of every ten I meet with. In manners, though your mighty strength and hatred of any meanness sometimes breaks out in violence – of which I must try to cure you, dear – in manners, if kindness, and gentleness, and modesty are the true things wanted, you are immeasurably above any of our Court gallants; who indeed have very little.

Having said that, it is probably quite useful, at least for Victorian readers, that King James gives John a knighthood shortly afterwards, and he marries Lorna to live happy ever after.

Or do they? For if one obstacle to John's marriage to Lorna is based on their differences in class, they also differ in the matter of religion. John is a Protestant, of course. Although he does not seem particularly devout, he is a member of the Church of England, attends the parish church of Oare, and is a church warden like his father before him. But Lorna is a Roman Catholic. Although her religion is not over-emphasised, it is gradually revealed that she is the daughter of the Roman Catholic Earl of Dugal, who, with his wife, had once visited Rome 'with a fervent longing for the Holy Father'. When Lorna joins the Royal Court of King James, she attends him at the celebration of Mass almost every Sunday, and John realises that he himself 'was not of the proper faith'. It is surely a comical irony, that when King James knights him, the King thinks John to be 'a good Catholic'. But John remains a Protestant and marries Lorna in his Anglican parish church.

It seems extraordinary that Blackmore should have made so little of these religious differences in a historical tale set around the years of the Monmouth Rebellion and the Glorious Revolution of 1688, precisely because of the violent disagreements over religion at that time. In the end, King James II was forced to abdicate because of hostility towards his Roman Catholic religion.

The fact is that Lorna's marriage to Sir John Ridd is a 'mixed' marriage, and as such was forbidden by her Roman Catholic Church, without special permission. Of this we hear nothing. Could an Anglican marry a Roman Catholic quite so easily in the late seventeenth century? So the question remains – was Lorna Doone really married?

11.

Whatever Happened to God in Children's Books?

From *The History of the Fairchild Family* to *Harry Potter and the Philosopher's Stone*

God, we have been informed, is dead, and no deader than in mainstream children's literature. In the past two hundred years, the overwhelming majority of children's books in English have moved from a religiously driven, primarily evangelical literature to a secular literature in which religious activity is feared, or not understood, or in which religion has become an empty cultural gesture.

One very striking example occurred in 2001 when there was a rumour that HarperCollins was planning to commission new Narnia titles. C.S. Lewis's series was (and is) a rare exception in the children's book market – one which (at least for three of the seven titles) wears its religious credentials on its sleeve. However, a strategy memo was leaked from HarperCollins: 'Obviously,' wrote an unfortunate executive, 'this is a biggie as far as the estate and our publishing interests are concerned.' But, he went on, 'we'll need to be able to give emphatic assurances that no attempt will be made to correlate the stories to Christian imagery/theology'. Christianity, it seems, had not merely vanished from children's books, but had become positively toxic.

How had this happened? Religion and faith have been replaced by myth and fantasy, and goodness is no longer reliable or an absolute. Take the central symbol of power and goodness, the father.

In Mrs Sherwood's highly influential *The History of the Fairchild Family* (1818-47), the relationship of father, mother, and children matches the relationship of God the Father, the Mother Church, and the congregation – the father represents God in his family, the mother interprets his words, and the children obey. It was a model for the structure of the Victorian

11. Whatever Happened to God in Children's Books?

Judy rushes to her godless death
in Ethel M. Turner's *Seven Little Australians* (1894);
illustration by A.J. Johnson.

family. As Mr Fairchild says to his son, 'I stand in the place of God to you, whilst you are a child; and as long as I do not ask you to do any thing wrong, you must obey me.' Therefore, the father may whip his son with a horsewhip (if only a small horsewhip) for not learning his Latin, but it is tough love, all to save the boy's soul. Two centuries later, things could hardly be more different. By 1990, in Gillian Cross's award-winning *Wolf,* the father is a terrorist prepared to kill his mother and daughter for some plastic explosive. In 2015, Deidre Sullivan's *Needlework* centres on a girl whose father has abused and raped her from the age of twelve. The father is not the reliable image that he used to be. J.K. Rowling, looking back at the first five Harry Potter books described them as 'a litany of bad fathers'.

Children's books always reflect, if sometimes in distorted and exaggerated ways, society itself, and here they seem to be reflecting the decline of religion and one of its major symbols.

Britain today, by most measures, is not a particularly religious (or traditionally religious) country. In January 2016, the number of weekly Church of England worshippers fell below 1,000,000 for the first time, and the Archbishop of Canterbury, Justin Welby, wrote in *The Guardian*:

> In some parts of the Communion the decline in numbers has been a pattern for many years. In England our numbers have been falling at about 1% every year since World War Two.... The culture [is] becoming anti-Christian, whether it is on matters of sexual morality, or the care for people at the beginning or the end of life. It is easy to paint a very gloomy picture.

In 2011, the Roman Catholic Church in Britain had the smallest number of priests since 1937, while evangelical churches are experiencing a revival. The third largest faith group in Britain, Islam, has around 2,000,000 practising members (an estimated 80 per cent of the total); overall, perhaps fewer than 8 per cent of the population actually practice a religion. However, it should be remembered that through the nineteenth century, the Anglican church's grip on its parishioners, in rural as well as urban areas, was never as complete as might be assumed.

And so, English-language children's books in the nineteenth century shifted slowly towards a secular fantasy and a pragmatic realism; this progressive loss of faith can be demonstrated in two best-selling, canonical, children's books, one from the USA and one from Australia.

In Louisa May Alcott's *Little Women* (1868) (and its sequel, *Good Wives* [1869]), the stresses between patriarchal power and child (or female) rebellion are clear to the modern eye. Mr March, the absent father, may still stand as God to his children, and Marmee is the present mother church, interpreting his word; the girls are 'little pilgrims' – they suffer, they pray, and, in *Good Wives*, one of them dies. But there is rebellion afoot. If we compare the narrator's tone when Beth dies, with that of Mrs Charlesworth describing her confident *Ministering Children* (1854) with their unwavering faith, then we see a world of difference. The reaction of Beth's rebellious sister, Jo, to Beth's death is portrayed with self-conscious authorial irony:

> Seldom, except in books, do the dying utter memorable words, see visions, or depart with beatified countenances. . . . Now, if she had been the heroine of a moral story-book, she ought at this period of her life to have become quite saintly, renounced the world, and gone about doing good in a mortified bonnet, with tracts in her pocket. But, you see, Jo wasn't a heroine; she was only a struggling human girl, like hundreds of others, and she just acted out her nature, being sad, cross, listless, or energetic as the mood suggested.

Ethel Turner's *Seven Little Australians* (1894), the Australian equivalent of *Little Women*, shows a world of even more distinctive independence, but now the physical father is brutal and unreliable, and the spiritual father quite absent. This book is almost a requiem for religion. At the end of the book, the rebellious female hero, Judy, is killed by a falling tree, and as she dies in the arms of her sister, Meg, we see the void left by the absence of the father and the loss of religion:

> Judy's brow grew damp, her eyes dilated, her lip trembled.
> 'Meg!' she said in a whisper that cut the air. 'Oh, Meg, I'm frightened! Meg, I'm so frightened!'
> 'God!' said Meg's heart.
> 'Meg, say something. Meg, help me! Look at the dark, Meg. Meg, I can't die! . . . Meg, I can't think of anything to say. Can't you say something, Meg? Aren't there prayers about dying in the Prayer book? I forget. . . .'
> Meg's lips moved, but her tongue uttered no word.
> 'Meg, I'm so frightened! I can't think of anything but "For what we are about to receive" and that's grace, isn't it? And there's nothing in Our Father that would do either. Meg, I wish we'd gone to Sunday school and learnt things. Look at the dark, Meg! Oh, Meg, hold my hands!'
> 'Heaven won't – be – dark,' Meg's lips said.

Even when speech came, it was only a halting, stereo-typed phrase that fell from them.

'If it's all gold and diamonds, I don't want to go!' the child was crying now. 'Oh, Meg, I want to be alive! How'd you like to die, Meg, when you're only thirteen? Think how lonely I'll be without you all . . . Oh, say something, Meg – hymns – anything!'

Half the book of Hymns Ancient and Modern danced across Meg's brain. . . . Then she opened her lips:

'Come unto Me, ye weary, and I will give you rest . . .'

'I'm not weary, I don't *want* to rest . . .'

There is now no father, no God, and no God the Father.

In the twentieth century, the overwhelming majority of mainstream writers of children's books ignore the Church totally. One exception is John Masefield, who so regarded the church as a social institution rather than something actively involved in human spirituality, that he felt that he could include the kidnapping of a Bishop and most of the chapter of Tatchester Cathedral in his cheerful farrago *The Box of Delights* (1935). Indeed, he seems to regard the Church as merely another ingredient in the kaleidoscope of English myth. One character, looking back over several thousand years of history, reflects in passing on paganism: 'That was our old religion. . . . It was nothing like so good as the new, of course'.

Arthur Ransome, perhaps the most influential of twentieth-century children's writers is more typical. In the Swallows and Amazons novels (1930-47) we find the age-old pattern of the absent, omniscient Father and the Mother who interprets his will to the children. There is a hierarchy within family, which is governed by good middle-class codes of behaviour. But the church is only mentioned in passing as part of the framework of society. The real articles of faith are adherence to codes – professional, family, cultural. Thus, when the children are in real danger in *We Didn't Mean to Go to Sea* (1937), sailing in storm and darkness across the North Sea, there is no reference to anything except self-reliance and acquired skills. The children's mantra is 'What would Daddy have done?'

One of the few exceptions to this secularisation was C.S. Lewis's partly allegorical Narnia series (1950-56), but the fact that it has had such wide and uncritical acceptance is taken by those who disapprove of Lewis's version of Christianity as evidence of the ignorance of the general population on matters of faith. Books that discuss Christianity seriously in a contemporary context, such as Aidan Chambers's *Now I Know* (1987), have become extremely rare.

Christianity, or, indeed, any religion, has become a minor, specialist area in terms of children's books; it has been replaced by at best a vague humanism. We have moved from a perhaps authoritarian confidence in religion as part of the fundamental thought processes of society to an era of fragmentation and uncertainty. Ultimately, as in Philip Pullman's *His Dark Materials* trilogy (1995-2000), we have arrived – literally – at the death of God.

More than that, the lack of sureness and faith has led to a deep unsureness about fiction. Take the example of *Harry Potter and the Philosopher's Stone* (1997), one of the most commercially successful children's books ever. The 'good' characters exemplify secular humanist values; the parents are lost; there is a quasi-omnipotent father-substitute; religion has been forgotten, domesticated. At the School of Magic they celebrate Christmas, but it is a secular, culturally commercial occasion with no significance beyond holiday and presents.

Curiously, perhaps, the Harry Potter books became for a while the most-banned books in the USA. The primary arguments against them rested, and rest, not simply upon a very naive understanding of the link between text and affect, but on the subject matter: those who would ban or burn the books fear the depiction of the occult *because they believe in it*. All of this is curious, for the books are the product of an age that (generally) understands that fiction is fiction. Non-believers – or believers in science – have not the slightest problem with Harry Potter: you cannot be corrupted by witchcraft, as it is a fiction. Rowling herself is reported as being 'truly bemused' by suggestions that she was advocating the occult.

I should like to stress that I am talking about 'mainstream' publishing. There are many specialist 'Christian' publishers – notably the successful Lion Hudson imprint who in 2015 produced *The Lion Comic Book Hero Bible* (in the style of Marvel Comics) – as well as publishers rooted in Islam (although apparently not many produce fiction) and other religions.

However, the cultural mainstream does not take kindly to proselytising – that is no longer what fiction is *for*. To take an example of a book for adults, Kel Richards's attempt to build religious arguments into detective novels in which the detective is one C.S. Lewis, such as *The Corpse in the Cellar* published by SPCK, received cool reviews. Unlikely to be reviewed at all are presumably well-selling series such as Jenny L. Cote's Epic Order of the Seven, published by specialist evangelical publishers. The first in the series, *The Prophet, the Shepherd, & the Star*, is perhaps most fairly summed up by the blurb:

> Side-splitting humor, danger, heartache, hope & spiritual truth.
> The Nativity Story – it's not just for Christmas anymore.
> A talking, musical scroll, a pigeon-flying-and-camel-driving

mouse, a writing cat, a courageous lamb, and two lion-fighting dogs provide non-stop action in this adventure that brings the Christmas story to life as never before. You will be astonished at the accuracy and perfection of the prophecies and God's unfolding plan to bring Jesus into the world.

But the gap between traditional Christian believers and unbelievers, as Archbishop Welby suggests, is very wide, and this text may be written in an incomprehensible language for many. Whether there is any going back to the sureties of the past, or whether children's books are (as they so often have been) accurate indicators of cultural movements – and they suggest that formal religion (at least Christianity) is in terminal decline – remains to be seen.

12.

Whose Side Was Henty really on in the American Civil War?

G.A. Henty, *With Lee in Virginia* (1895)

The political views of G.A. Henty (1832-1902), the Victorian writer of boys' adventure stories, are pretty well known. He spent the first half of his life serving in the army during the Crimean war and then working as a Special Correspondent for the *Standard* newspaper. He devoted his later years to writing colourful adventure stories for boys in which he extolled the achievements of the British Empire. A life-long Tory, his literary career coincided with the high tide of imperialism, and he produced a whole stream of historical tales with such titles as *With Clive in India; or, the Beginnings of an Empire* (1884) and *With Buller in Natal; or, A Born Leader* (1901). Although many of these stories focus on episodes in British history, Henty was widely travelled, and often dealt with exciting events in other countries. *The Young Franc Tireurs and their Adventures in the Franco-Prussian War* (1872) is about two boys' adventures in France, while *For the Temple: A Tale of the Fall of Jerusalem* (1888) deals with the Jewish Revolt in early Christian times.

Henty knew America well. He wrote no fewer than five full-length stories about it, including *True to the Old Flag: a Tale of the American War of Independence* (1885) and an early 'Western', *Redskin and Cowboy: A Tale of the Western Plains* (1892). In 1895 he published *With Lee in Virginia: A Story of the American Civil War*, and from what we know of Henty we would expect him to be a supporter of the Confederate side and the South in the conflict. This suspicion is confirmed when in his Preface to Scribner's American edition of the book, Henty confessed that 'I have written this story from the Confederate point of view.'

Messrs. BLACKIE & SON'S PUBLICATIONS

Still the Most Popular Boys' Favourite

G. A. HENTY

Popular 3s. 6d. Edition

Extra crown 8vo.   Fully illustrated

111 **At Aboukir and Acre:** The French in Egypt.
119 **At Agincourt:** The White Hoods of Paris.
126 **At the Point of the Bayonet.**
43 **Both Sides the Border:** Hotspur and Glendower.
138 **The Bravest of the Brave:** Peterborough in Spain.
30 **By England's Aid.**
65 **By Pike and Dike:** Rise of Dutch Republic.
1 **By Right of Conquest:** or, With Cortez in Mexico.
64 **Captain Bayley's Heir.**
44 **The Cat of Bubastes:** A Story of Ancient Egypt.
23 **A Chapter of Adventures.**
7 **Condemned as a Nihilist:** A Story of Escape from Siberia.

Bestselling imperialism:
a Blackie's flyer for G.A. Henty (1867).

12. Whose Side Was Henty really on in the American Civil War?

The main plot of *With Lee in Virginia* is one of Henty's most interesting and skilful. In telling the story of his young hero, Vincent Wingfield, the son of a Virginian planter who becomes a scout in Robert E. Lee's army of the South, Henty not only gives his readers the usual mixture of dash, danger, heroic exploits, imprisonment, and escapes, but he handles Vincent's moral development with a sophistication that his stories do not always reveal.

To begin with, although fifteen-year-old Vincent is always a likeable character, he is often thoughtless and impulsive. Although we admire his generous impulses, we can see that he lacks judgement. When the Civil War starts and Vincent joins the Confederate army, he begins to learn to combine his lively spirit with more prudence, and his sisters notice that he seems to have become much older in manner and appearance. When he is captured by Unionist soldiers, his escape demonstrates not only his courage and ingenuity, but also his care and thoughtfulness in his relationship with Lucy Kingston, the young girl who initially nursed him when he was wounded.

He has already tried to prevent a slave from being beaten and tried to help a victimised slave's wife. Promoted to the rank of captain, Vincent is involved in spying operations for General Lee. But he realises that the defeat of the South is imminent and he begins planning for the future – persuading his mother to free their slaves immediately, and to give them land and wages for their work. At the end of the story, Vincent marries Lucy and becomes master of the estate who is due reward not only for his bravery but also for his gradual growth and maturity, and for his moral qualities. Vincent is one of Henty's most sustained attempts at the depiction of character development, and the attempt is not without some success.

The social context of Vincent's story is, of course, the plantation life and slavery in the Southern states of America. It is clear, despite his professed sympathy for the South, that Henty is attempting to be fair and objective. He goes out of his way to praise the magnanimity of the Union generals, such as Grant and Sherwood, as well as criticising the irresponsibility and cruelty of some slave-owners. But, while not uncritical of the worst aspects of slavery – he denounces physical violence and the separation of families – he basically defends it as a tolerable social system, and suggests that Negroes are at least as well off as the lowest classes in Europe at the time. His view of slaves is essentially that of the sentimental stereotype. The Negroes are 'very like children and indulgence spoils them', says Mrs Wingfield, the sympathetically presented mother of the young hero. The reader is told that the slaves' condition is better than Europeans because 'the climate was a lovely one'. (Over 37º in the summer months!) The widespread cruelty, the sexual exploitation of female slaves and the appalling living conditions are simply passed over. Not least, Henty ignores the fact that people may actually prefer political freedom, with the risk of lower living standards, than having higher standards under a political tyranny. In all this Henty seems to be reflecting the complacent views, not only of many Southerners but of the Victorian England of which he was such a forceful and popular representative.

But Victorian England, as we know, was in fact bitterly divided over the issue of slavery in America, and often countered economic arguments with more humane considerations. Many people were also proud of the fact that, led by such men as William Wilberforce, Britain had succeeded in abolishing slavery throughout the British Empire as early as 1833. In discussing this division of opinions in Britain over the American Civil War, the great historian Élie Halévy, in his *History of the English People in the Nineteenth Century*, described the situation in the following terms: 'So far as generalisations can be made, upper-class opinion and opinion in South England favoured, without necessarily approving the Southern cause. Radical, middle-, and working-class opinion was strong for the North.' As an example of this, the cotton-workers of Manchester at a mass-meeting in 1862 urged President Lincoln to prosecute the war and abolish slavery despite the fact that the Union's blockade of Lancashire trade was causing them hardship; and in January 1863, Lincoln wrote a famous letter to thank them for their 'sublime Christian heroism'.

Although Henty overtly professed to support the Southern cause, when we examine the narrative structure of his story about the American Civil War, we can see how it actually reflected those divided feelings in Britain about slavery. The main plot in Henty's story, as we have seen, is concerned with Vincent Wingfield's career and moral development as a slave-owner and soldier. But this is accompanied and almost paralleled by a subplot about slaves and slavery in a way that surely reflects the unease felt by Henty and swathes of British society about the treatment of slaves in America. Indeed this subplotting is done with such skill and emphasis that it threatens to undermine Henty's whole *apologia* for the South. There is a tension throughout the novel between Henty's professed attitude towards slavery and a subplot that poses challenging questions about it.

From the first chapter, Vincent Wingfield's adventures involve him directly with slaves, and we see him intervening to help Dan to escape from a beating. From then on a story emerges that runs throughout the whole novel, revealing the sufferings but also the courage and ingenuity of the slaves, and which contradicts the stereotype of them as child-like, lazy and well-treated. This subplot about slavery is so strong as to occupy a substantial part in sixteen of the book's twenty chapters.

12. Whose Side Was Henty really on in the American Civil War?

After the initial episode involving Dan in the first chapter, the next three chapters deal with the slave, Tony, who is brutally treated by his owner, Jackson. In fact, Jackson sells off Tony's wife, Dinah, in order to punish him, but she is bought by the kindly Wingfield family and becomes their loyal servant, nursing Vincent when he is wounded in the war. Vincent also helps Tony to run away to the north after another flogging. The slave, Dan, who helps Vincent to escape from the Union prison in chapter ten, accompanies him on the long journey south; and the ex-slave, Tony, now a sergeant in the Union army, helps Vincent escape again when he is caught spying and is likely to be executed. There is a clear parallel and symbolism present in those contrasting episodes where Vincent helps the slave to escape in chapter three, and the same slave helps Vincent to escape in chapter nineteen.

Throughout the stories of the two Negro slaves Dan and Tony, and the sufferings of Tony's wife, Dinah – sold and separated from her husband in chapter two, and kidnapped in chapter fourteen – Henty reveals a strikingly different picture of slavery from his overtly expressed opinions, and one that directly challenges those simplistic and over-optimistic views. You could say that in a story full of journeys, while the *main plot's* journeys deal with the battles of the Civil War, the *subplot's* journeys deal with Vincent's escape from prison and his attempts to free slaves. The structure of the book oscillates between battle-journeys in support of slavery and secession, and slave-journeys in support of abolition and freedom.

It was by its stamina and robust energy that Victorian Britain was able to contain so many contradictory impulses within itself and yet prosper, and it is this same stamina and energy which Henty reveals in his novel about the American Civil War. Although he tried to write a story in favour of the Confederacy and the South, G.A. Henty may really have been on the side of the Union without knowing it.

13.

What Do Children's Books Do about Christmas?

In this secular and commercialised age, certain religious festivals lure even the best publishers to break otherwise well-entrenched rules about religious neutrality in children's books. Religion can be a tricky business, and, as we have seen, it has drifted out of the mainstream of English children's books. But Christmas seems to be the exception: the financial temptation is too great. As the great Tom Lehrer said, 'Christmas, with its spirit of giving, offers us all a wonderful opportunity each year to reflect upon what we all most deeply and sincerely believe in – I refer of course, to money.'

There is nothing new about this – the mishmash of symbols and rituals that has accumulated around the festival are, of course, a mixture of tradition, religion, commercialism, and chance. The now ubiquitous Christmas tree (one feels almost like dropping the capital letter) arrived in England via a circuitous route from Germany around 1829, and was then popularised by Prince Albert and Queen Victoria in 1841; the Christmas card dates from around 1844. Then there is that curious hybrid Father Christmas himself: the varied Saint Nicholas legends crystallised most significantly into Clement Clark Moore's *The Night Before Christmas* (1823), a poem currently available in Britain in at least twenty editions – and, inevitably, perhaps, in the form of *The Zombie Night Before Christmas*. You can also buy the Coca Cola Santa Claus version: Santa had worn a red coat before the 1931 Coca Cola advertising campaign, but Haddon Sundblom's paintings for that campaign have fixed the image – and Sundblom did derive some of his inspiration from Moore:

13. What Do Children's Books Do about Christmas?

The image of Christmas:
Thomas Nast's 'Merry Old Santa' (1881).

He was dressed all in fur, from his head to his foot,
And his clothes were all tarnished with ashes and soot.
A bundle of Toys he had flung on his back,
And he looked like a peddler, just opening his pack.

His eyes – how they twinkled! his dimples how merry!
His cheeks were like roses, his nose like a cherry!
His droll little mouth was drawn up like a bow,
And the beard of his chin was as white as the snow.

The stump of a pipe he held tight in his teeth,
And the smoke it encircled his head like a wreath.
He had a broad face and a little round belly,
That shook when he laughed, like a bowlful of jelly!

Then there is the Dickensian Christmas feast, encapsulated in *A Christmas Carol* (1843): it is difficult to estimate, but there are probably more than fifty editions of that book currently in print in English, including one by the Marvel Comics Group – surprisingly faithful to the original text. And perhaps oddest of all is *Rudolph the Red-Nosed Reindeer*, originally written by Robert L. May, a copywriter for the American department store Montgomery Ward. It was given away as a publicity item in 1939 (2.5 million copies) and again in 1945 (3.5 million copies). (The song, as an example of the quirky areas into which research can lead you, was written by May's brother-in-law, Johnny Marks, and Gene Autry's version was not only the first number one hit of the 1950s, but also the only number one to have dropped immediately out of the chart.) The book is, curiously, difficult to find today.

Children's books about Christmas have, as it were, snowballed, and have thrown up some noteworthy oddities, such as Dr Seuss's *The Grinch Who Stole Christmas* (1957) and Raymond Briggs's groundbreaking, and typically iconoclastic *Father Christmas* (1973). But beyond these, every major publishing group – and almost every publisher – has its stable of Christmas franchises, and until you have looked into the lists the jaw-dropping level of exploitation may not be obvious. The mystery becomes, 'Is the market saturated? How much more can it possibly take?'

Those children's book characters who have a Christmas book devoted to them include Angelina, Babar, Arthur, Harry Horse's Little Rabbit, Splat the Cat, Thomas the Tank Engine (including *Thomas's Night Before Christmas* and – now branded as 'Engine Adventures' – *The Last Train for Christmas*). Then there is Mrs Pepperpot, Felicity Wishes (*Little Book*

13. What Do Children's Books Do about Christmas?

of Christmas), Peppa Pig (*Peppa Pig and the Lost Christmas List*), Ernest and Celestine, Postman Pat (who has a lot of snow problems), Fireman Sam (*The Runaway Santa, Christmas in Pontypandy*), Shirley Hughes's delightfully middle-class Lucy and Tom, and Alfie and Annie Rose; Judith Kerr's Mog, and Sally Hunter's Humphrey (a character familiar to those who shop in Mothercare).

We are just beginning. Topsy and Tim *Meet Father Christmas*, Sarah and Duck (spinning off a CBeebies animated series) have *Christmas Lights*, Paddington has *a Christmas Surprise*. Take a breath. There's Pat Hutchins's *It's Christmas, Titch*; *Horrid Henry's Christmas Play*; *Happy Christmas, Spot*; Mandy Stanley's *Lettuce: a Christmas Wish*; *Hello Kitty – Merry Christmas*; and even *Curious George's Christmas Countdown*. Possibly the award for marketing chutzpah should go to the Mr Men franchise, which not only has *Mr Men: The Christmas Party*, *Mr Men's Christmas Carol*, and *Mr Men's 12 days of Christmas*, but which invented new characters – Little Miss Christmas, and, of course, Mr Christmas. Even the supremely talented Janet and Allan Ahlberg could not resist another outing for their inter-textual hero with *The Jolly Christmas Postman*.

There are Christmas carols, mice, parades, goodnights, cookies, magic, snow, plays, and wombats (naturally). Christmas is saved by Little Reindeer, Polar Bear, and perhaps improbably (or inevitably) by Norman the Slug.

Not only do famous authors get on the bandwagon – *Richard Scarry's Christmas Tales*, *Michael Morpurgo's Christmas Stories*, *Enid Blyton's Christmas Stories* – but authors and celebrities jump on too: Richard Curtis's *The Empty Stocking*, Mariah Carey's *All I want for Christmas is You*, to name but a couple. It seems that every celebrity and their dog (or wombat) has some Christmas kitsch.

Is nothing sacred? Well, apparently not, and I am not referring to religion. Thus we find Emma Thompson's continuation of the Beatrix Potter 'franchise', *The Christmas Tale of Peter Rabbit* (2014), while Andrew Grey has added to the annals of Winnie-the-Pooh with *Pooh's Christmas Adventure* and *Pooh's Christmas Letters*.

Some titles are inexplicable (*Dinosaur vs Santa*), some look as though they have comic potential (*Santa's Stuck*), and some, it seems to me, may push the limits of tolerance even of those who have the most residual attachment to the dignity of the festival. *Rudey's Windy Christmas* by Helen Baugh and Ben Mantle – about one of Santa's reindeer who has eaten too many sprouts – may be cheerfully vulgar; and Nicholas Allen's *Father Christmas Needs a Wee!*, in questionable taste; but for many Tom Fletcher, Dougie Poynter, and Garry Parsons's *The Dinosaur That Pooped Christmas!*, may represent turning-the-face-to-the-wall time.

For the vast majority of authors and publishers Christmas seems to have become only a general excuse for giving presents and being nice to each other. But, aside from the specialist Christian publishers (who, for an inexplicable reason tend to produce unstylish, not to say amateurish illustrations) there *are* examples of the nativity story being told simply with beautiful artwork – by Brian Wildsmith and Ian Beck, for example. (On the other hand, Julie Vivas's *The Nativity*, with text from the 1662 Bible and illustrations of the archangel Gabriel with tattered multicolour wings and wearing scruffy boots has been banned in some sensitive areas of the world.)

Much of the most interesting work has been the attempt either to narrate the nativity from a new viewpoint or to create new mythologies. In the first category we might find Michael Morpurgo and Quentin Blake's account of the first shepherd to see the infant Christ, *On Angel Wings*; Brian Wildsmith's *A Christmas Journey*, in which Mary's pet dog and cat follow her to Bethlehem; Martin Waddell's *Room for a Little One* (in the stable); or Catherine Storr's *The Donkey's Christmas Story* (an 'easy piano picture book' with ten carols to play). Even the whimsical can work here, as with Nicholas Allen's *Jesus' Christmas Party*, centring on the landlord of the inn at Bethlehem who can't get to sleep what with all the shepherds and angels . . . On the other hand, Geraldine MacCaughrean and Ian Beck's *The Little Angel* (' "I'm afraid of flying," said the little angel. "And I'm terrified of wolves," said Micah the shepherd boy') hinges, as it were, on the theologically problematical idea that an angel can have a broken wing.

Attempts to create new, but religiously centred mythologies can be more successful, such as *A Small Miracle*, by the underrated Peter Collington. An old lady, who lives alone in her gipsy caravan, passes a church that has just been raided by a thug on a motorcycle. She rearranges all the crib figures, and then, on her way home is knocked down by the thug. As she is freezing to death in the snow, the crib figures come to life, pick her up, carry her to her caravan and light the fire and prepare her food. *The Christ Child and the Spiders* by Jan Peters and George Buchanan has the Christ Child (aged about 10) enter a sleeping house on Christmas Eve; he finds that all the spiders have been banished to the attic and allows them to come downstairs to look at the tree. As he leaves, they cover it with their sparkling webs. In both cases, outlandish as their premises may be, there is an underlying consciousness of, and respect towards, the spiritual season.

Many of the books cited above are steeped in nostalgia for Christmases past – or that perhaps were never past – snow, carols, and the England of Thomas Hardy. As Kenneth Grahame illustrates at his more lyrical in *The Wind in the Willows*:

13. What Do Children's Books Do about Christmas?

> It was a pretty sight, and a seasonal one, that met their eyes when they flung the door open. In the fore-court, lit by the dim rays of a horn lantern, some eight or ten little field-mice stood in a semicircle, red worsted comforters round their throats . . . and forthwith their shrill little voices uprose on the air, singing one of the old-time carols that their forefathers composed in the fields that were fallow and held by frost, or when snow-bound in chimney corners, and handed down to be sung in the miry street to lamp-lit windows at Yule-time.

The fact that the carol that follows is explicitly Christian (' "Who were the first to cry Nowell?" / Animals all, as it befell') in a book that is in places quite explicitly pagan is perhaps characteristic of the contradictions involved here.

Thus Christmas is both celebrated and not celebrated in *Harry Potter and the Philosopher's Stone*; it becomes a parable, as in the accounts of the Christmas truce of 1914 (*The Best Christmas Present in the World* by Michael Morpurgo and Michael Foreman, and *The Christmas Truce: the Place where Peace was Found*, by Hilary Robinson and Martin Impey); and its characters are becoming wildly intertextual – Father Christmas guest stars in books as disparate as C.S. Lewis's *The Lion, the Witch and the Wardrobe* and Julia Donaldson's mega-selling *The Stick Man*.

The confusion that is Christmas, with its plethora of mixed messages, and its increasingly obscured core of belief is, sadly perhaps, accurately reflected in children's books, as so many things are.

14.

Is Little Lord Fauntleroy a Children's Story – and Does the Subplot Work?

Frances Hodgson Burnett, *Little Lord Fauntleroy* (1886)

*L*ittle Lord Fauntleroy was well received from its start when it was serialised in *St. Nicholas,* the American paper for children, from November 1885. When it was published in book form by Scribner's in New York and Warne in London in 1886, it became one of the best sellers of the year, and was soon translated into more than a dozen languages. Frances Hodgson Burnett's stage version of the novel two years later was successfully produced in England, France, and America, and ran on Broadway for four years. The book's popularity, furthermore, encouraged sales of a wide variety of by-products, such as Fauntleroy toys, playing cards, writing paper, and chocolate. Most notoriously of all, the book created a fashion for Little Lord Fauntleroy suits made of black velvet with lace collars, in which enthusiastic parents dressed their unwilling children all over Europe and America. It was this fashion foisted upon reluctant children, more than the actual story, that made Little Lord Fauntleroy somewhat unfairly a by-word for a 'sissy'.

The reasons for the book's popularity are fairly obvious. The story of Cedric's rise from being a poor American boy to becoming a wealthy English aristocrat is a typical use of the rags-to-riches formula, and the story also includes a tyrannical Earl, comic characters, a sensational subplot involving a criminal conspiracy, and a strong attack upon social injustices in the Earl's treatment of his workers and tenants.

The origins of the story are clear. By the autumn of 1884 Mrs Hodgson Burnett, who, although born in Manchester, England, was living with her family in America and had published a number of successful adult novels, when her two small sons asked her to write a children's book. 'Why don't

14. Is Little Lord Fauntleroy a Children's Story?

Cedric settles in:
illustration by Reginald B. Birch for Frances Hodgson Burnett's
Little Lord Fauntleroy (1886).

you write some books that little boys would like to read?' asked her younger son, Vivian; and she was so amused by Vivian's interest in American politics and his curiosity about the English aristocracy that she decided to write a story about him. She described her thought process in 'How Fauntleroy Occurred' in 1898:

> I will put him in a world quite new to him and see what he will do. How shall I bring a small American boy into close relationship with an English nobleman – irascible, conservative, disagreeable? He must live with him, talk to him, show him his small, unconscious republican mind. He will be more effective if I make him a child who has lived in the simplest possible way. Eureka! Son of a younger son, separated from ill-tempered noble father because he married a poor American beauty. Young father dead, elder brothers dead, boy comes into title! How it would amaze him and bewilder him! Yes, there it is, and Vivian shall be he – just Vivian with his curls and his eyes and his friendly, kind little soul. Little Lord Something – or other. What a pretty title – Little Lord –, Little Lord –, what? And a day later it was Little Lord Fauntleroy.

The family had lived for some time in New York, where Vivian had befriended their local grocer, and then moved to Washington where the young schoolboy became a strong supporter of the Republican party. The description of Cedric wearing his black velvet suit with a lace collar was based upon a photograph of Vivian taken in the summer of 1885. Mrs Hodgson Burnett sent this photograph to Reginald Birch as a suggestion for the illustrations of *Little Lord Fauntleroy*. Clearly she used many aspects of her son Vivian's life in her story about an American boy's becoming an English lord.

But is it really a children's story?

Although born in England, Frances Hodgson had moved to America in 1865, where she began to earn a living writing stories for the popular magazines. But she had gradually become a successful and serious adult novelist, with such books as *That Lass O' Lowrie's* (1877) and *Through One Administration* (1883). She came to be regarded as one of America's leading writers alongside W.D. Howells and Henry James, and she was much admired by Mark Twain.

But she had not written any books for children before, and, although it is clear that *Little Lord Fauntleroy* was initially written for her two young sons and serialised in a children's magazine, there are elements in the story that raise questions about its status as a children's book. One might, for example, wonder whether a plot that concentrates on the suitability of a young American woman's marriage to the son of an Earl across strict class barriers in the Victorian Age is an interesting topic for a children's story, and whether it might not be more appropriate for an adult best seller.

Indeed the irony Burnett achieves by her use of a dual-narrative voice in the story suggests that she was addressing adults as much as child readers. This is the way in which, while telling her story to children, she occasionally portrays events that children might not understand. On the voyage from New York to England, for example, Cedric makes friends with some of the sailors, so that his conversation acquires a nautical flavour at times, and he makes the other passengers laugh when he uses such expressions as 'Shiver my timbers, but it's a cold day!' Cedric is surprised when the passengers laugh at this, for he is quite unaware of being comical, and adults smile at his innocent precociousness. There are more instances of this when Cedric arrives at Dorincourt Castle and he makes a footman smile when he offers to help the crippled Earl to walk; and he later questions the Earl about wearing his coronet, making one of the servants turn aside and cough in order to avoid laughing aloud. The most striking example of this dual-narrative voice, of course, occurs when Cedric consistently praises the irascible Earl's kindness, although his tenants and servants know that the truth is the opposite. He is 'such a good Earl,' writes Cedric to his friend Mr Hobbs. 'He reminds me of you he is a unerversle favrit [*sic*].'

It looks, in other words as if Mrs Hodgson Burnett is writing a book that addresses both children and adults. It is not solely a children's book, but what is sometimes called a 'cross-over' book that appeals to adults as much as it does to children. Cross-over books are not a modern phenomenon, of course. *Alice's Adventures in Wonderland* is an earlier example. What Mrs Burnett is doing, whether consciously or unconsciously, is writing a story that is aimed at adults as well as children. This phenomenon has become popular in recent times, when books by such authors as Philip Pullman and J.K. Rowling are published with different covers for their adult and child readers. Louis M. Alcott, the famous author of *Little Women* (1868), recognised this cross-over phenomenon in an enthusiastic review of *Little Lord Fauntleroy* published in *The Book Buyer* in December 1886 where she wrote, 'Grown people who still love children's books will enjoy much which escapes the young reader in the working out of the fierce old Earl's regeneration, which is a fine piece of work.'

The subplot, however, is another matter.

Subplots are a common feature of many stories. In addition to the main plot, the author adds a secondary narrative that often parallels aspects of the main plot. In *King Lear*, Shakespeare uses the subplot about the Duke of Gloucester and his loyal son Edgar to contrast with the treatment of King Lear by his daughters. In *David Copperfield,* as well as telling his main story about David and Dora and Agnes, Dickens also tells us of many other marriages, such as Mr and Mrs Micawber, Barkis and Peggotty, and Dr and Mrs Strong.

In *Little Lord Fauntleroy*, the subplot is about the criminal conspiracy to replace Cedric as the Earl's true heir by a false claimant. It might be said to parallel the main plot since it also concerns parents and a missing child.

Cedric, it will be remembered, is the son of Captain Cedric Erroll, third son of the Earl of Dorincourt. When the Earl's two older sons die, one in a riding accident, the other of a fever in Rome, Cedric unexpectedly becomes the Earl's heir and so Lord Fauntleroy. Despite his initial doubts and misgivings, the irascible old Earl gradually comes to love his grandson Cedric. But the Earl's lawyer Mr Havisham brings news that, before he died, Bevis, the Earl's eldest son, had married and produced a son by his wife Minna. This son is the true heir, and he, not Cedric, is the real Lord Fauntleroy.

The Earl is heartbroken by this dramatic news. But, back in America, before he had become Fauntleroy, Cedric had befriended a young bootblack named Dick. Dick and Cedric's old friend, Mr Hobbs, the grocer, become concerned when they learn that Cedric is no longer heir to the Earl. But one of Dick's customers gives him an illustrated paper containing a picture of the young claimant's mother, whom Dick instantly recognises as Minna, the wife of his older brother Ben. This information is quickly passed on to Mr Havisham, the Earl's lawyer, and he is able to successfully reinstate Cedric as the true heir. He does this by proving that Minna's marriage to Bevis was bigamous, as she was already married to Ben; her son's father was Ben, not the Earl's eldest son. So Cedric regains his title as Lord Fauntleroy, and Ben's son, Tom, is restored to his father.

We can see that the subplot of *Little Lord Fauntleroy* – involving the minor characters Dick, Mr Hobbs, Ben, his wife Minna and son, Tom – mirrors the main story, with its group of fractured family relationships and their restoration. Tom returns to his father as Cedric returns to his grandfather. But the means by which this is achieved is unconvincing melodrama. Dick's recognition of his sister-in-law's photograph in a paper so fortuitously given to him by a passing customer, and who also happens to be a helpful lawyer, strains credibility. We have to say that there is an enormous difference of skills, almost an artistic gulf, between the ways Mrs Hodgson Burnett handles the main story and the subplot in her popular book.

15.

Why Was Billy Bunter never really Expelled from Greyfriars School?

The Magnet (1908-40)

Discipline seems to be pretty strict at Greyfriars, the fictitious public school invented by Frank Richards, which is the alma mater of Billy Bunter. There are plenty of rules about behaviour and school work and serious offences such as bullying, drinking, gambling, and stealing. They are backed up by a series of sanctions, which are administered by Doctor Locke, the Headmaster, and his teachers, including the Remove's form master, Mr Quelch and the Prefects. They use various punishments ranging from requiring the boys to write impositions or inflicting beatings with a cane (which are often called floggings) to rustication and complete expulsion. 'Flogging' seems to be a somewhat flexible term, ranging from six strokes by a Prefect to a flogging by Dr Locke, which sounds altogether more painful.

These sanctions are employed quite frequently. Canings and impositions occur in numerous episodes of the *Magnet*, and, it has to be admitted, the boys seem hardly the worse for them. Caning seems to be an almost universal punishment, and on one occasion Mr Quelch gives Bunter no fewer than thirty strokes on his backside, without this seeming to inflict any lasting damage. Famously, Mr Quelch is regarded as 'a beast but a just beast'.

The ultimate sanction against seriously bad behaviour is, of course, expulsion, with the offending boy being permanently dismissed from the school and sent back to his parents or guardian. This is by no means an uncommon punishment, and over the years quite a few miscreants are expelled from Greyfriars.

Billy Bunter in his prime,
as illustrated by Charles Henry Chapman between 1911 and the 1970s.

15. Why Was Billy Bunter never really Expelled?

The worst offences seem to be cheating, drinking, gambling, and theft; sexual misbehaviour, rather oddly, given what is said to go on in many public schools, is never mentioned at Greyfriars. In the most striking episode when heterosexual activities do threaten to appear, Wingate, the captain of the school, who falls in love with a visiting actress, arranges to meet her outside school and loses all interest in school activities, which even includes dropping out of the school football team. But when Dr Locke discovers this, he treats him not with punishment or threatened expulsion, as you might expect, but with sympathy and understanding.

Real cads are severely punished, of course, and over the years a number of boys leave Greyfriars under a black cloud, such as Carberry, a bullying blackguard who drinks and gambles; Gadsby and Snaith, who are thieves; and Ernest Levison for persistent rule-breaking. The boy most deserving of expulsion is Rupprecht von Rattenstein, who commits all kinds of unpleasant offences, and is finally expelled for forging a letter to a book-maker in the name of the honest and upright hero, Harry Wharton.

With Greyfriars being run as it is, many readers must have asked themselves the question: 'Why was Billy Bunter never fully expelled from Greyfriars?'

He is always in trouble, of course, and often punished. Bob Cherry, Harry Wharton, and the rest of the boys in the Remove have the full measure of Bunter's selfish antics and don't let him get away with much. Mr Quelch and the other masters often punish him for his deceit, laziness, and general ill-behaviour, too. Readers might wonder what offence he has to commit to be expelled permanently. There are, however, a few occasions when Bunter is expelled from Greyfriars School, but for so short a period as to be easily forgotten or overlooked by many readers. In 1924, for example, in *Magnet* issues 874-877, Bunter was expelled for playing tricks with his ventriloquism, but he refuses to leave the school and forms a one-man picket outside the school gates until his sentence is quickly rescinded. In 1930 he is briefly rusticated, but that is to prevent him revealing details of a police investigation, and he rejoins the school as soon as the case is completed. In *Magnet* issues 1374-1382, in 1934, he is again briefly expelled for boasting of a crime really committed by Fisher T. Fish, but the rest of the Remove protest his innocence, and with their support, and that of Mr Quelch, Bunter is soon reinstated. In a TV programme from 1954 called *Bunter Must Go*, Bunter was again expelled briefly for apparently hurting Mr Quelch, but refuses to leave the school and is pardoned when Coker confesses to the crime. His expulsions always seem to be brief and easily passed over.

How serious, then, are Bunter's crimes, we have to ask. When he first appears he does not seem too bad. On his first appearance in the opening issue of the *Magnet*, he is described as 'a somewhat stout junior, with a broad, pleasant face and an enormous pair of spectacles'. But over the years from 1908-40 we get to know him better. He is greedy and lazy and snobbish, always boasting of non-existent aristocratic and rich relations, and unpleasant to scholarship boys such as Mark Linley. He lies, particularly when trying to borrow on the strength of forthcoming postal orders, which, of course, never arrive. He is cowardly when any danger threatens but always willing to pick up confidential information by eavesdropping or peering through keyholes. His presence in class is always likely to be disruptive because of his foolishness and his lies, often told to impress people.

The trouble is that Bunter's tricks and lies are so palpably obvious as to invite ridicule, and the comedy arises from the gulf between Bunter's ambitious deceits and the inept way in which he tries to carry them out. Here is the Fat Owl of the Remove trying to explain why he did not steal another boy's cake – his knowledge of the circumstantial details and his contradictions make his guilt quite obvious:

> 'I say, you fellows –' he gasped.
>
> 'What have you been up to, you fat villain?' asked Harry Wharton.
>
> 'Nothing,' answered Bunter promptly. 'You fellows know whether I'm the sort of chap to bag a fellow's cake.'
>
> 'Oh, my hat!' ejaculated the three together.
>
> 'Of course, I never went into Smithy's study at all,' explained Bunter. 'I never saw him bringing the cake from the tuck-shop, never saw him take it into his study, and never waited behind the door in Study No. 7 till he went out again. The fact is that I was talking to Toddy in the gym, at the time.'
>
> 'Oh, crumbs!'
>
> 'Being in the library at the time – I mean the gym! – naturally I never knew anything about Smithy's cake,' explained Bunter with dignity. 'Knowing nothing whatever about it, however could I have snaffled it? I ask you!'

Bunter, we can see, is an almost Falstaffian figure of comic greed, cowardice, and deceit. He is boastful, vain, devious, and lazy, but he is not a vicious character like Rupprecht von Rattenstein. There are even occasions when he is positively kind, such as when he befriends a young vagrant called Flip, who has run away from the criminal underworld, and

15. Why Was Billy Bunter never really Expelled?

Harry Wharton & Co., the Famous Five, were always around to show Bunter the error of his ways with a sound walloping —BUMP! "YAROOOH! BEASTS! I SAY —CRIKEY!"

The Greyfriars chums, from a souvenir edition of 1965.

whom Bunter finds a place for in the second form at Greyfriars. This is why, although they recognise his faults and rag him mercilessly for them, his fellow Removeites are prepared to defend Bunter when he is real trouble, as they do in 'The Popper Island Rebellion' – a sequence of stories – in 1934, when they bar themselves out of the school onto Popper's Island because they believe in Bunter's innocence.

The truth is that Bunter cannot be permanently expelled from Greyfriars, whatever he does, but this is for purely dramatic reasons. He became so important not only for his role in some of the labyrinthine plots but because his comic presence is a vital element in the ethos of the stories. He makes Greyfriars what it is. Although Frank Richards may never have intended Bunter to become such a great figure when he first appeared in the *Magnet*, he gradually became an indispensable (and un-expellable) force. It is significant that when, after World War II ended, and Frank Richards began to publish full-length stories, not serials, about Greyfriars in 1947, the publishers felt it necessary to include Billy Bunter's name in the titles of all thirty-three books that followed, such as *Billy Bunter's Banknote* (1948) and *Billy Bunter at Butlin's* (1961). He had become one of the immortals. As George Orwell said, in his famous essay on 'Boys' Weeklies': 'Bunter . . . is a real creation. His tight trousers against which boots and canes are constantly thudding, his astuteness in search of food, his postal order which never turns up, have made him famous wherever the Union Jack waves.'

16.

Why on Earth Are there Children's Books about War?

When it comes to children's books, everyone should be allowed to be mystified about something that is not a mystery to anyone else. And this is my personal mystery.

Of course, the obvious answer to the question 'Why on earth are there children's books about war?' is – 'Why on earth not?' It is straightforward enough to argue that *every* subject is a fit one for children's books, and that children (as a group) are intelligent enough to be self-regulating about what they read. If parents or other guardians have strong views, then they are able to do the regulating. It also seems to me that although children's books are too often a place of retreatism for adults, they should not be so for children. Thus I have always agreed with the great illustrator Edward Ardizzone – both a portrayer of idyllic childhood and a war artist, when he said,

> I think we are possibly inclined, in a child's reading, to shelter him too much from the harder facts of life. Sorrow, failure, poverty, and possibly even death, if handled poetically, can surely all be introduced without hurt. . . . If no hint of the hard world comes into these books, I'm not sure that we are playing fair.

War is, to put it mildly, 'one of the harder facts of life'; war is all around us, and, it sometimes seems, increasingly so. There are, if we take the definition currently adopted by the United Nations, at least ten major wars happening at the moment, and in 2014 *The Independent* estimated that only eleven countries in the world were *not* involved in war of some kind.

16. Why on Earth Are there Children's Books about War?

A dangerously unrealistic version of war
from the prolific Percy F. Westerman (1917).

It is hardly surprising, then, that war infuses, directly or indirectly, many children's books; war is there, but how and when do we mediate it to our children? And, basically, as Eric Kimmel, an award-winning American children's author, has said, 'To put it simply: is mass murder a subject for a children's novel?' For some – quite a few – writers, the answer to that question is yes: Gudrun Pausewang's *The Final Journey* (*Reise im August* [1992/1998]) is a book that ends in a gas chamber. The First World War is well-trodden territory, from Percy F. Westerman's chillingly unrealistic *A Lively Bit of the Front* in 1917 to Michael Morpurgo's all-conquering *War Horse* (1982) and *Private Peaceful* (2003). Similarly, so is World War II: in 2016, *The Guardian* reviewed Sandi Toksvig's *Hitler's Canary* (2005) (set in wartime Denmark), and *Anna and the Swallow Man* (2016) by Gavriel Savit (fantasy in wartime Poland). Modern warfare is not neglected: Carnegie winner Robert Westall wrote a psychological fantasy about the Gulf War (1990-1), entitled *Gulf* (1992), almost before it had finished; recently there has been *Girl on a Plane* (2015) by Miriam Moss (a girl captured by the Popular Front for the Liberation of Palestine in the 1970s) and, if not directly about war, Gillian Cross's *After Tomorrow* (2015) fictionalising the plight of refugees.

But I am still worried that, when it comes to naturalism/realism, war might be a special case, because of questions of empowerment and disempowerment. In my experience, many people who deal with children and books feel that children can deal with everything except complete hopelessness. The distinguishing essence of a children's book, it might be said, is that it in some ways empowers children, the weakest members of society, and this seems to apply, however bleak the situation portrayed. Anne Fine, author of a number of grim black comedies, such as *Madame Doubtfire* (1987), put it this way:

> Children are powerless . . . absolutely powerless. And so . . . the one thing I try and do . . . is to give children a sense that, even though these cataclysmic things happen . . . that it's not as bad as they think or even if it is as bad as they think they will somehow come to terms with it. . . . If the children's writer has a job, it is to interpret the world to the child. You may bring some comfort.

And yet, I wonder whether even such a bleak view is valid in the case of war, total or local. My father once told me that when war was declared between Britain and Germany in 1939, the overwhelming response among ordinary people was one of relief – even a kind of light-headedness that responsibility had been taken away from them. To be disempowered meant the lifting of a burden. Higher powers, for good or evil, were in control.

If we interpret 'realism' in fiction as relating in a direct way to the real world, we are usually dealing with topics where the child at least has a chance of being *actually* empowered. Real children do survive divorce, they do survive drugs – there is somewhere to go. And, of course, children survive wars – even holocausts. But in the case of war, adults are disempowered too: if we tell children a story in which even the adults are disempowered, what hope of power is there for the children? That kind of realism is such that there can be no escape in real life, and no retreat into fantasy in fiction.

Barbara Harrison, an American academic, has pointed to the key issue:

> although there is now greater candour in literature for the young than ever before, the one characteristic which adults are reluctant to see diminished in any way is hope, traditionally the animating force in children's books. Many adults cannot endure the thought that during the Holocaust, hope . . . was swept into the ovens.

I am quite aware that I have a weak logical case here, and that my personal, deep fear of helplessness is edging in (not that I mind that, because, as no less than D.H. Lawrence pointed out, all criticism and all responses to literature must be ultimately personal), but I think that it remains an important puzzle for the writers of children's books about war.

One of the major fantasy and science fiction writers of the twentieth century, Ursula K. Le Guin, has discussed the question of presenting 'realism' in books for children, and war might be seen to be the ultimate form of realism:

> I agree that children need to be – and usually want very much to be – taught right from wrong. But I believe that realistic fiction for children is one of the very hardest media in which to do it. . . . Or you get 'problem books'. The problem of drugs, of divorce, of race prejudice . . . and so on – as if evil were a problem, something that can be solved, that has an answer, like a problem in fifth grade arithmetic. If you want the answer, you just look at the back of the book.
>
> *That* is escapism, that posing evil as a 'problem'. . . .
>
> But what, then, is the naturalistic writer for children to do? Can she present the child with evil as an *insoluble* problem. . . . To give the child a picture of . . . gas chambers . . . or famines

or the cruelties of a psychotic patient, and say, 'Well, baby, this is how it is, what are you going to make of it' – that is surely unethical. If you suggest that there is a 'solution' to these monstrous facts, you are lying to the child. If you insist that there isn't, you are overwhelming him with a load he's not strong enough yet to carry.

That is the crux. I know that many will argue for the almost mystic ability of fiction to mediate these impossible premises – but for me, the subject of war brings us close to the limits of fiction. If I am reading about what would be *otherwise* unimaginable horrors – whether they are in Vietnam (for example, Rachel Anderson's *The War Orphan* [1984]) or in the Middle East (for example, Lynne Reid Banks's *One More River* [1973]) – then I have a problem. I seriously wonder whether my horror is not horror in response to the dramatic fiction of war (such as in Tolkien's *The Lord of the Rings* [1954-5]), but that it is a response to the reality *behind* the fiction – a reality that is *masked* by the fiction, rather than revealed by it. Fiction – even realistic fiction – seems almost to trivialise, to falsify in this case. Intuitively, I seem to think that war is all too serious to be fictionalised.

Or, of course, if you have faith in fiction, then you could argue that fiction can say the unsayable, increase our response, add metaphorical depth, or symbolic coherence – and, in your support, I quote Joseph Kessel:

> Events on a grand scale, mass sufferings, catch the imagination and arouse compassion only incompletely and in an abstract way. We need a specific example to arouse our love or fear. We are so made that the face of a weeping child touches us more than hearing that a whole province has died of starvation.

Again, that may be true, but is it a justification of fiction? As I have said, I know that I have a weak case because I am in danger of devaluing *all* fiction. And yet, I still suspect that war is, in the emotions of many, a different case.

Or maybe it is simply too late. Do our media-saturated children have a different understanding of war than my lucky (born just post- World War II) generation? Worse, has the distinction between fiction and reality – especially in television coverage of wars – become blurred? The problem is not simply that fictionalised war has become an entertainment – for it always has been, from the earliest oral epics. It is more that the non-book media – the dominant forms of media – have packaged real war as fiction to the point that what is *actually* going on is unimaginable. What place, then, does fiction have?

One example this can be found in Terry Pratchett's *Only You Can Save Mankind* (1992) – and if anyone is likely to modify my general view of war books, it is Pratchett. He begins with the premise that war is incomprehensibly horrible, and then deals with my central problem – of how to make sense of this. The second thing that makes these books more acceptable to me than most on the subject is that they are really about my own problem – that of understanding war. Pratchett deals with the reactions of contemporary teenagers to it, and in doing so, makes the point (to them) that they do not, and perhaps cannot, understand. *Only You Can Save Mankind* is a peace parable. Johnny Maxwell is drawn into a computer game in which he finds that the aliens he is supposed to eliminate have feelings too. Meanwhile, in parallel 'real life', the first Gulf War is being reported on the television, but it only impinges on Johnny obliquely: 'There was a film on the News showing some missiles streaking over some city. It was quite good.' The children discuss the war in adult terms, but it is only Johnny, who thinks differently about things, who sees the problem. One of his friends says,

> 'I mean – the whole world seems kind of weird right now. You watch the telly, don't you? How can you be the good guys if you're dropping clever bombs right down people's chimneys? And blowing people up just because they're being bossed around by a looney?' [And another says] 'There was a man on [the television] saying that the bomb-aimers were so good because they all grew up playing computer games'.
>
> 'See?' said Johnny. 'That's what I mean. Games look real. Real things look like games. . . . We always turn [war] into something that's not exactly real. We turn it into games and it's not games. We really have to find out what's *real*.'

My point, really. We turn war into fiction, into a game, until we can't tell the difference.

But, finally, *why* would anyone choose to write about these things? Surely, my inner, honest self asks, there are nicer, more cheerful things to give children? Are there better ways to build a better world? I am not anti-historical – the dangers of forgetting are obvious enough – but fictionalising these major human catastrophes may carry the danger that they *become fiction*.

Most of the answers that I have found to the question 'Why would anyone choose to write about these things?' are highly principled and optimistic. Barbara Harrison sums them up. Writing about war books published in the USA, she noted,

> The books are important documents for historians and for social and political scientists. . . . But we must acknowledge at the outset . . . the quintessentially moral nature of these books. They instruct: they seek to make people better than they are. . . . A tragic work of art deals with human aspiration and suffering, and it examines with profound seriousness the place of the individual in the universe.

Kate Agnew and Geoff Fox in *Children at War* are similarly optimistic:

> In the treatment of the two world wars in recent novels and picture-books . . . young readers are invariably urged to examine the nature of violence and suffering, persecution and endurance, hatred and loyalty, selfishness and sacrifice. They are asked to share the writers' condemnation of war and the repugnant beliefs which lead to conflict, and to feel compassion for the anguish imposed upon the innocent many by the powerful few.

All the authors Agnew and Fox looked at shared 'a passionate belief':

> children must be made aware of the evils of the past and the courage with which that evil has often been met; and also that young readers need narratives which explore the nature and experience of war if they are to make sense of the world they have inherited and the future they confront.

If that were true, I would have no unease, but such high-mindedness is not, I am afraid, always evident in mainstream children's publishing, let alone in the bloodthirsty, jingoistic comic books and the manic slaughter of computer games and summer blockbusters.

I am left with the mystery: because it cannot plumb the depths of adult fiction, is war fiction for children *necessarily* disrespectful of the real dead?

17.

Biggles: Tough Guy or Romantic Hero?

W.E. Johns, *The Camels Are Coming* (1932), *Biggles Buries a Hatchet* (1958), and *Biggles Looks Back* (1965)

For the casual reader of stories by W.E. Johns about his great flying hero, Biggles, the question of Biggles's sexuality might well arise. Biggles, or Captain James Bigglesworth, to give him his proper name, seems to have had no female acquaintances during his long and adventurous career from his days as a pilot in World War I and World War II to his subsequent exploits after the war as a flying detective. This intrepid flying ace, the kind of figure one imagines to have always had a drink in one hand and a pretty girl on his arm, seems to have enjoyed the company of men only.

First, there is his cousin, the Honorable Algernon Lacey (always known as 'Algy'), who joined him in World War I as a trusted lieutenant, and Flight Sergeant Smyth, his skilful and reliable mechanic. Then in stories after that war, Biggles is joined by a more youthful companion, Ginger Hepplethwaite, 'a lad of fifteen or sixteen years of age', a working-class character whom Biggles encourages to join a flying school and then enlists to become a valued colleague. During and after World War II Biggles often adds more socially diverse comrades to his team, such as 'Tex' O'Hara from the USA and 'Tug' Carrington, a tough cockney, but the one major and enduring new member of the team proves to be Lord Bertie Lissie, a silly-ass type hero with a monocle. Is Biggles just a man in a man's world, where women are simply below the radar?

More thorough readers of the Johns canon know otherwise. True Johns aficionados will have read a very early story about World War I, 'Affaire de Coeur', a magazine story that was republished in the book *The Camels are Coming* in 1932. In this sad tale, Johns depicted the young pilot Biggles

Some of Biggles's First World War exploits,
first published in 1934, and reissued in the 1970s.

falling passionately in love with the French woman Marie Janis, whom he met when he made a forced landing in his Sopwith 'Camel' aircraft during the war. She is described as 'a vision of blonde loveliness, wrapped up in blue silk'. When Biggles first meets her, he says, 'I've been looking for you all my life. I didn't think I'd ever find you.' They begin an affair, but Marie turns out to be a German spy. She does genuinely love Biggles, however, and tries to redeem her betrayal by protecting him from a planned bombing raid. Tragic circumstances intervene, and Biggles comes to believe that she has been killed in the war. He never forgets her.

Years later, well after World War II, Biggles comes to befriend his former German enemy, Erich Von Stalheim. They had long been fierce opponents. Stalheim, a formidable German agent, had clashed with Biggles before World War II in such stories as *Biggles Flies East* in 1935 and *Biggles and Co* in 1936. Not surprisingly, they found themselves on opposite sides in World War II, in such stories as *Biggles in the Baltic* (1940) and *Biggles Defies the Swastika* (1941). After the war, however, Von Stalheim is imprisoned in a Russian prison camp on Sakhalin Island, and ironically Biggles is sent by the British government to rescue him because he knows the whereabouts of a top-secret missing Russian missile. This is narrated in *Biggles Buries a Hatchet* in 1958, and so we learn how the two former enemies become allies and friends.

In *Biggles Looks Back* of 1965, the two friends meet again and reminisce about the old days. 'Did you ever wonder what became of Marie Janis?' Von Stalheim asks, and Biggles replies: 'I've never stopped wondering.' Van Stalheim reveals that Marie did not die during the bombing raid in World War I, as Biggles believed. She not only escaped, but in fact survived to serve as a German spy in World War II. Now she is living as a prisoner in a mysterious Bohemian castle in Czechoslovakia.

'There has never been another woman in my life,' Biggles tells Von Stalheim, and he plots to rescue her from this castle in communist-ruled Eastern Europe. After various thrilling adventures, Biggles – with the help of Algy, Bertie, and Ginger, and, of course, Von Stalheim – manages to get her to safety to England. And there Biggles continues to support her in a cottage in the Hampshire village 'where she now lives, Biggles and Von Stalheim often running down for the weekend to talk of their many adventures'.

Biggles is not simply a tough, clinical automaton: he is a romantic hero, like Sydney Carton in Charles Dickens's *A Tale of Two Cities* (1859), tragically loyal to the only woman he ever really loved.

18.

Why Is there Nobody Nice at St Clare's?
Enid Blyton, *The O'Sullivan Twins* (1942)

This question is, I hasten to add, not my question – and I hasten to add that because the girls' school story is one of those areas of children's literature (and there are many) into which the uninformed critic strays at his (and in this case, definitely *his*) peril. Given that the books were written to be read by young females, and that in many cases those young females have developed into older females with an enviable expertise in what is a huge field, the last person whose opinion might be considered even slightly valid would be an aging male who has not read many of the books in the genre. I have a great deal of sympathy with that point of view: Rosemary Auchmuty point outs out in the Preface to *The Encyclopedia of Girls' School Stories* (edited by Sue Sims and Hilary Clare) that while children's literature has had enough trouble establishing itself as worthy of intelligent study, girls' stories in particular have had to fight for recognition, even by so-called experts. And so one (and especially this so-called expert) should approach this topic with due humility – and beware of extrapolating generalisations from limited evidence!

Enid Blyton's school stories form a small part of her massive oeuvre, but, as one might expect from the professionals' professional, she includes all the right ingredients – midnight feasts, the bully, the sneak, the dramatic rescue, the funny French teacher, the firm-but-fair Headmistress, and so on; all very familiar, and we might assume – indeed, critics generally do so assume – comforting or reassuring. There is no question that she was, and is, successful – the books are still in print after seventy-five years, and in our house her two major series – Malory Towers and

18. Why Is there Nobody Nice at St Clare's? 95

The great days of the girls' school story:
The School Friend in 1936 – with a guest appearance
by Bessie Bunter, Billy's sister.

St Clare's – were read to pieces, literally, by my four daughters to the extent that some of the volumes had to be replaced, rather like hamsters, several times.

Because I am professionally involved with children's books, childhood books stay on the shelves in our house, even after the daughters have left; but when they come back with their families to stay, they return to their books and I find copies of *Little House on the Prairie* or *Betsy-Tacy* left on the bedside tables or in the bathroom.

On one of these occasions, our youngest daughter (in her late twenties) came down to breakfast with a disintegrating copy of *The O'Sullivan Twins* (I have since discovered two more copies about the house) and asked the question, 'Why is there nobody *nice* at St Clare's?'

And so, in the name of research, I read it. The O'Sullivan twins, Pat and Isabel who, in the first of the six-volume series, *The Twins at St Clare's*, learned to love their new school, return in this book for the second term, and a term of, it seemed to me, almost unremitting unpleasantness. This time there are three new misfits. The first is the twins' cousin, Alison, who is not exactly treated with loving consideration, even before she makes her entrance:

> 'I wish Alison wouldn't smile that silly smile so much' [said Pat].
> 'Oh, I expect some one has told her what a sweet smile she has or something,' said Isabel. 'Really she seems to think she's a film-star, the way she behaves!'

Of course, they are only imitating their father; as he says, with that moderation that age always brings, 'Well, if you can make that conceited little monkey into somebody nice, I shall be surprised. I never saw any one so spoiled in my life.'

By the end of the book, Alison 'was really learning to be much more sensible' but not before she has been thoroughly humiliated by the fifth-formers because she doesn't know how to light fires, among other salutary experiences. She gets no sympathy from her classmates:

> She went back to the common room, sniffing, hoping that every one would sympathize with her.
> But to her surprise, nobody did – not even kind-hearted Lucy Oriell. Pat looked up and asked her what was up.
> Alison told her tale.
> 'Fathead!' said Janet in disgust. 'Letting down our form like that! Golly, the big girls must think we are mutton-heads.'

> 'It was *awful* being rowed at by so many of the big girls,' wept Alison, thinking that she must look a very pathetic sight. But every one was disgusted.
> 'Stop it, Alison. You're not in kindergarten,' said Hilary. 'If you want to behave like an idiot, you must expect the top-formers to treat you like one . . .'
> Janet lost her temper. 'Either stop, or go out,' she said roughly to Alison. 'If you don't stop I'll put you out of the room myself. . . .'
> [Alison] stopped crying at once, and the twins grinned at each other.
> 'Lesson number one!' whispered Pat.

This tough love (as we might charitably call it) is not extended to the second misfit, Erica, and even the narrator does not approve of her: 'she really was a sneak. Not even the mistresses liked her.' We never find out what motivates this unfortunate character: the girls punish her for telling the teachers about their illicit midnight feast (and, worse, not owning up to it), she is not allowed to go into the town, and nobody will speak to her. 'She would have a bad time! It's hard to see glances of contempt and dislike wherever you look, and have nobody saying a jolly word.'

Later on, it is discovered that she has framed Margery (the third of the victims, of whom more in a moment) by spoiling Pat's books and allowing Margery to take the blame. How do the first-formers react – with the loving-kindness and understanding that we might expect from well-bred (or at least well-heeled) young ladies? Well, not quite:

> the girls were intensely angry when they heard that it was Erica who had spoilt Pat's jumper and books – and had allowed the blame to rest on Margery.
> 'The beast. The hateful beast!'
> 'I'd like to pull her hair out! . . .'
> 'Oh, the spiteful creature! I'll never speak to her again as long as I live.'
> 'Just wait till she comes back into class! I'll give her an awful time.'

All this bonhomie is interrupted by the 'good' character, Lucy (who has the advantage of having 'dancing black curls, and . . . deep blue eyes that sparkled and shone'), who explains that poor Enrica was scared and unhappy. She then says goodbye to the scared and unhappy Enrica, 'who dreaded all that her mother would say', with the encouraging words, 'Now you just tell your mother honestly that you've been a mean and spiteful girl.' That should fix things.

And so, as the narrator somewhat dismissively explains,

> poor, mean little Erica disappeared from St Clare's to start again somewhere else. Nobody missed her, and nobody waved to her as she went down the school drive in a taxi with her trunks. She had made her own punishment, which is always much harder to bear than any other.

As for Margery, that poor girl, who has a sad backstory ('nobody cares about me at home, so I'm miserable, and I'm always badly behaved when I'm miserable') is immediately categorised when she arrives as a 'tall bad-tempered-looking girl', and is treated accordingly. True, the other girls attempt to be nice to her (for a time) but after Margery has a row with their history teacher, Miss Lewis, they turn on her:

> 'I think Margery ought to have been expelled from the school! After we'd tried so hard to be decent to her too. You simply CAN'T help a girl like that.'
>
> So once more Margery was sent back to her lonely, friendless state. No one spoke to her if they could help it, and nobody even looked at her.

Given that there is clearly something wrong, do our heroes, Pat and Isabel, stand up for her and help? Actually, no: they deliberately make things worse. On the day of the big lacrosse match, Pat goes into the changing room – and doesn't realise that Margery is there:

> 'Now, don't forget, everybody, if that miserable Margery shoots a goal, we don't clap and we don't cheer. See?'
>
> 'Right, Pat,' said the others. 'She doesn't deserve even a whisper – and she won't get it.'
>
> 'You horrid beast, Pat!' said Margery, suddenly standing up in anger. 'So that's what you've planned to do have you! Just like you! . . .'
>
> The bell rang for the players to take their places. Margery went on to the field, a tall and scowling girl.
>
> 'I'm sorry for the girls she's got to play against!' said Belinda to Rita. 'My word, she's an extraordinary girl.'

Not a word to suggest that Pat's behaviour might not be exemplary.

Margery, fuelled by righteous anger, plays amazingly – 'She ran like the wind, she tackled fearlessly, she caught accurately. . . . She was a miracle of swiftness as she darted about the field, tackling and dodging, getting the ball when it seemed impossible.' Afterwards, Pat feels 'a bit uncomfortable . . . about not cheering her a bit' – but that's as far as her sympathy and human kindness goes. In any case, as she says of Margery, 'It's this meanness I can't stand. . . . I can put up with bad manners and rudeness and even sulkiness, but I just hate meanness.' Margery has to become the Heroine of the Fire, bravely rescuing the craven Erica before her virtues can be recognised.

But we are not quite at the end, as there is always time for the girls to scare the gullible (and French) Mam'zelle into a nervous breakdown. Such fun! And how culpable are the staff? Although they are in charge, the pleasant-faced form mistress, and of course, Miss Theobald, the headmistress, she of the 'calm, serious face' and with a 'compassionate glance in her deep eyes', seem to be able to do little about this behaviour.

No need to worry, though: all is forgiven and away the girls go for the Easter holiday, 'and reunions with dogs and cats and horses at home'. Margery is going to stay with the sainted Lucy, which is, of course, lucky for her. As Lucy says, 'We shan't have any maids or anything, because we are poor now, but Margery's going to help in the house all she can – isn't she a brick?'

The problem from an outsider's point of view (and this applies to boys' school stories as well) is that *The O'Sullivan Twins* – and, my daughters assured me, once they had thought about it, most other books of the same type that they had read – refutes a part of the well-established theory as to why school stories are popular. Fictional schools, it is thought, provide a safe space for children to work out real-life problems through fiction; tensions are contained, and the texts, by having nice people in them who overcome the bad people, are comforting and comfortable. This is why C.S. Lewis was sceptical about school stories in his essay 'On Three Ways of Writing for Children': 'I do not mean that school stories . . . ought not to be written. I am only saying that they are far more likely to become "fantasies" in the clinical sense than fantasies are.'

That is, they will become mere wish fulfilment.

After some reflection, a breakfast committee of daughters concluded that C.S. Lewis was diametrically wrong. The St Clare's stories, looked at coldly, are *not* fantasies, but raw realism. Girls, together (they said), *are* horrible; perhaps nobody is nice at St Clare's because we have to face the fact that in the school environment, few people are nice at all. The books are *not* the place where readers can emulate the admirable, or identify with the underdog, and where all comes right in the end. Rather, they are places where girls (or boys) can work their revenge on the great and the good and the self-satisfied – where, rather than being the-new-girl-who-triumphs, we can be in the gang, and bully the outsiders, just as we are bullied ourselves. The only fantasy in *The O'Sullivan Twins* (apart from the displacement fantasy of the reader being an insider at a posh school) is that things end happily for the misfits. (Well, most of them.)

Speaking as a father whose only experience of a girls' secondary school has been watching school concerts, attending prizegivings, and verbally fencing with teachers on open evenings, I can but bow to my daughters' superior knowledge.

19.

Were there Two Flutes?
Time Present and Time Past at Green Knowe

L.M. Boston, *The Children of Green Knowe* (1954)

Lucy Boston's life was almost as remarkable as her children's stories. Born in Southport, Lancashire, in 1892, she went up to Somerville College, Oxford, in 1914 to read Classics, but left after two terms to train as a nurse and served in a French hospital during the Great War. She married in 1917, and after the war she travelled a good deal in Europe, writing poetry, and pursuing a career in the Arts. Her marriage broke down in the 1930s, and with her son, Peter, she settled in Cambridge. Then in 1939 she bought an extraordinary Manor House in the village of Hemingford Grey. Reputedly the oldest continuously inhabited house in Britain, it had been built around AD 1130, and Mrs Boston set to work to restore it to its original state and planted a beautiful garden round it, notable for its exquisite topiary and fine collection of old roses, and lived there until her death in 1990. This is the place renamed in her books as Green Knowe.

Yew Hall, Mrs Boston's first novel, was published in 1954 (when she was over 60), the same year in which she also produced the first of the children's books on which her reputation largely rests. This was *The Children of Green Knowe*, the story of a young boy called Tolly, and his visit to his great-grandmother, Mrs Oldknow, at her ancient home of Green Knowe, where he enjoys adventures with the children of earlier occupants of the house from the seventeenth century. *The Chimneys of Green Knowe* followed in 1958, a story about Tolly's return to his great-grandmother's at Easter when he comes to know the two children of the house who lived there in Napoleonic times: Susan, a blind girl, and Jacob, a Negro slave boy. In *The River at Green Knowe* (1959), two visitors, Dr Maud Biggin and her friend

Sybilla Bun, have rented Green Knowe for the summer, and invite three children – Ida, Oskar, and Ping – to come for their holidays, and they have various adventures as they explore the river, including meeting a winged horse and discovering a live giant. *A Stranger at Green Knowe*, published in 1961, is about Hanno, a gorilla, who escapes from London Zoo to Green Knowe, where he is befriended and protected by the little Asian boy, Ping. *An Enemy at Green Knowe* (1964) is about the struggle between Mrs Oldknow and a malignant witch, Dr Melanie Powers, who lays siege to the house before Tolly and Ping help to defeat her. *The Guardians of the House* (1974) is about a boy named Tom and his exploration of the house to try and identify various objects, such as a straw mask, an unusual vase, and a stone head, which help to defend it – they are its guardians. Finally, in *The Stones of Green Knowe* (1976), the last book in the series, which is set in AD 1120, Mrs Boston's new hero, Roger, watches his father rebuild what was a Saxon house as a Norman Manor, and in the process meets the occupants of the house – Toby and Linnet from the seventeenth century, Jacob and Susan from the Napoleonic era, and Tolly from the present day.

It is clear that Mrs Boston uses her depiction of the house of Green Knowe, with its river and its beautifully atmospheric garden, to explore a wide range of thematic interests, such as the difference between the real and the supernatural, the delicate relationships between children and adults and each other, and the plight of 'displaced' people, such as Oskar and Ping. (Even Hanno the gorilla, wrenched from the tropical forests of the Congo to England, is an example of displacement.) Mrs Boston's stories celebrate the glories of the natural world, and ask fascinating questions about time.

The treatment of time, change, and continuity, and the ways they interact with each other are at the heart of her stories about the house of Green Knowe, the Norman Manor House she acquired so fortuitously in 1939 and lived in till the end of her life in 1990. Her books proclaim the persistence of characters and events, particularly if they are enshrined in a special place. Thus the Green Knowe of the twentieth century carries within it forces, spirits, values, often in the form of what might be called 'friendly ghosts', which have survived from the past, and are still alive, to be encountered by later generations.

> Time present and time past
> Are both perhaps present in time future,
> And time future contained in time past.
>
> – T.S. Eliot, *Four Quartets*

19. Were there Two Flutes?

Alias 'Green Knowe' – the ancient and atmospheric Manor at Hemingford Grey, on the Great Ouse near Huntingdon.

The Stones of Green Knowe proclaims this most eloquently. Roger, the eleven-year-old son of the Norman lord Ormond d'Aulneaux, watches the stone masons and builders skilfully transfer his father's Saxon hall into a Norman Manor, using stones specially brought from a quarry in the Midlands. But apparently by contact with two great stone chairs that Roger stumbles upon in a clearing in the forest, he finds himself transported into a wood where he rescues an eight-year-old girl from being attacked by a violent ruffian. She proves to be Linnet, who with her brother Toby, belongs to the seventeenth century. Roger realises that contact with the great King Stone enables movement forward in time, and contact with the Queen Stone enables movement backwards, and so he decides to make a brief visit to the earlier Saxon era. He also meets Susan and Jacob from the Napoleonic period and Tolly from the twentieth century, thus spanning a gap of 850 years. Somehow all these children, or their ghosts – Toby, Alexander, Linnet, Susan, Jacob, Roger, and Tolly – survive in the great house of Green Knowe, but they also know that must fight to preserve it. 'Oh my house,' Roger thought. 'Live forever!'

It is not always easy to keep a grip on these movements through time, as when, for example, the reader learns that the beautiful young girl whom Roger meets with Tolly in chapter 10 proves to be Tolly's own grandmother. It is not surprising that Roger finds his head reeling as he tries to comprehend his discoveries.

The Children of Green Knowe, the first book in the series, is perhaps the most enchanting. Schoolboy Tolly is sent to spend his Christmas holidays with old Mrs Oldknow, his great-grandmother at her home of Green Knowe. He hears mysterious noises in the house – strange creakings, boys' laughter, the neighing of a non-existent horse; and when he leaves a sugar lump for the horse, it disappears. But Mrs Oldknow has an oil painting over the fireplace of a seventeenth-century family – two ladies and three children, Toby, Alexander, and Linnet, and gradually Tolly discovers that these same children are still real presences in the house, whom he meets and plays with.

Alexander is a gifted musician – good enough to sing at Court for King Charles II – and wants to become a poet, and when Tolly first meets the children he hears Alexander playing a flute. Earlier in the story, however, Tolly had found a toy box in his bedroom in which he discovered Alexander's old flute. When his great-grandmother suggested that he should play it, he hesitates:

> 'Alexander has got it,' he says. 'How can there be two of it?'
> 'The one he has now is part of him,' Mrs Oldknow says. 'This is one he used to have. It is like a snakeskin when the snake sloughs it off.'
> But Tolly is not convinced. 'No, Granny. This is Alexander's flute. It's the real one. I know it is not a flute-skin.'

Eventually Tolly does learn to play Alexander's flute and seems to be reassured, when, during a later encounter with the ghostly children, Alexander says that he has given the flute to him, as if he has been able

19. Were there Two Flutes?

to transfer the flute away from the seventeenth century across time into Tolly's twentieth-century world. (It is rather like the way Hatty's skates move from the nineteenth century to the twentieth in Philipa Pearce's story, *Tom's Midnight Garden*.) Yet Alexander continues to play his flute in the seventeenth century, as we find when we read *The Stones of Green Knowe*.

The mind-blowing question, then, is this: could there possibly be two flutes in the *Green Knowe* books, one of which is still being played by Alexander in the seventeenth century, and one played by Tolly in the present? For if Alexander really does give his flute over the years to Tolly, it means that decisions made in the past not only influence the present, but might retrospectively be able to alter the past itself.

20.

Why Does C.S. Lewis Annoy so many People?
The Chronicles of Narnia (1950-6)

Given that C.S. Lewis's Narnia series of fantasy novels has sold between 65 and 100 million copies in thirty to forty-seven languages (depending on your sources), it might seem a little perverse to bring this up. His books, as even his most vociferous critics admit, tell good (read: page-turning) stories, and the film franchise, although it has stuttered, continues to be a success. Even though the first novel, *The Lion, the Witch and the Wardrobe*, is more than sixty years old, it has worn surprisingly well, when many other novels of its era have become period pieces. And it is not simply popular acclaim from child readers. Writers of religiously themed novels for the young are few and far between, and Lewis and his children's books have been enthusiastically adopted by everyone from fundamentalist evangelicals to the non-religiously aligned, who regard them as being particularly respectable and 'safe'. (One suspects that Lewis almost certainly would not have enjoyed either of these scenarios.)

Leaving the popularity of his children's books aside, children's book scholars have every reason to be grateful to him; in an academic world that was positively hostile to children's books, he took them seriously, producing two of the best early essays on the subject. In 'On Three Ways of Writing for Children' (1952), he put forward dicta that have become, in certain circles, basic tenets for thinking about children's books, the most famous of which is 'I am almost inclined to set it up as a canon that a children's story which is enjoyed only by children is a bad children's story. The good ones last. A waltz which you can like only when you are waltzing is a bad waltz.'

20. Why Does C.S. Lewis Annoy so many People?

Master of Narnia:
C.S. Lewis (1898-1963).

His argument is that, as an adult, 'I now enjoy fairy tales better than I did in childhood; being now able to put more in, of course I get more out.' It all sounds very sensible: children's books are just as important as adult books, and should be taken seriously.

He also provided one of the best ever defences for those adults who are criticised for reading children's books:

> Critics who treat *adult* as a term of approval, instead of as a merely descriptive term, cannot be adult themselves. To be concerned about being grown up, to admire the grown up because it is grown up, to blush at the suspicion of being childish; these things are the marks of childhood and adolescence. . . . When I became a man I put away childish things, including the fear of childishness and the desire to be very grown up. . . . They accuse us of arrested development because we have not lost a taste we had in childhood. But surely arrested development consists not in refusing to lose old things but failing to add new things.

He even seems to give children priority: 'We must of course . . . hope that we may do them good. But only such good as involves treating them with respect.'

This idea of having respect for the child reader also occurs in the essay 'Of Stories' (1947): 'Our superiority [over children] consists partly in commanding other areas, and partly . . . in the fact that we are better at telling stories than they are. The child as reader is neither to be patronized nor idolized: we talk to him as man to man.'

He also puts the case for the wholehearted author, one who is not consciously designing a book for a specific audience – and this is an idea that has become a widespread ideal for children's writers:

> I am not quite sure what made me . . . feel that . . . a fairy tale addressed to children, was exactly what I must write – or burst. Partly, I think, that this form permits, or compels you to leave out things I wanted to leave out. It compels you to throw all the force of the book into what was done and said.

He argues that he does not care for just the action: 'For I wanted not the momentary suspense but that whole world to which it belonged.' Children's books are not just a succession of thrills.

He continued, in another essay, 'Sometimes Fairy Stories May Say Best What's to Be Said' (1956): 'I was therefore writing "for children" only in the sense that I excluded what I thought they would not like or understand; not in the sense of writing what I intended to be below adult attention.'

Respect for children, respect for stories, a deep desire to write, great skill as a religious apologist, great skill as a storyteller. So, what's not to like?

As it happens, the world of Narnia was not popular even as it was conceived. Lewis's friend, J.R.R. Tolkien, creator of the meticulously detailed and consistent fictional world of Middle Earth, objected to Lewis's random plundering of traditional materials for his stories. In *The Lion, the Witch and the Wardrobe* there is the obvious Christian allegory, alongside creatures from a variety of mythologies – giants, centaurs, dryads and naiads, fauns – and even Father Christmas.

As might be expected, in this secular world, Lewis's religious beliefs have come in for some criticism – and it is curious that this has often been combined with personal criticism. His popularity with (especially) American evangelicals is undimmed – the C.S. Lewis Institute was founded in 1976 with its headquarters in Springfield, Virginia, which 'endeavours, in the legacy of C.S. Lewis, to develop disciples who will articulate, defend and live their faith in Christ in personal and public life'. But even this is rather surprising. As an evangelical commentator, Mike Duran, observed recently:

> C.S. Lewis is still considered one of the greatest Christian theologians, thinkers and authors of all time. But why? Of course, disbelieving in the innerancy of Scripture is far more serious than smoking tobacco and swilling suds. But nowadays a Christian author/thinker who smoked cigarettes, drank beer, believed in evolution, felt compelled to pray to Apollo, and rejected biblical innerancy would have about as much chance of becoming an evangelical hero as Paris Hilton does of becoming relevant.

One of the major objections is that the theology implied in the books is one of predetermination – that the very thing that contemporary children's books would place almost above all, free will, is denied the characters. Philip Pullman disliked Lewis (and Tolkien) because they were Platonists:

> They saw this world, this physical universe, as a fallen state, created, no doubt, by God but marked and weakened and spoiled by sin. . . . Well, I passionately disagree with this. The physical world is our home: this is where we live; we are not creatures from somewhere else or in exile.

It is only fair to say that a good many good people have sprung to Lewis's defence, perhaps most notably Dr Rowan Williams, latterly the Archbishop of Canterbury. In *The Lion's World: A Journey into the Heart of Narnia* (2012), Williams provides an eloquent, indeed, formidable, and formidably scholarly defence: 'Narnia brings into clear focus a wide variety of central Christian themes . . . Lewis's aim is to help us sense what the experience of God is "like", as if we had never thought about it.'

However, even he has to admit that all is not well: 'Lewis cannot by any means be wholly acquitted of the racial and cultural prejudices of his day; and he does not have to be beyond fault to be admired and loved.'

Others have not been so tolerant.

One of the earliest critics to take serious objection to Lewis was the distinguished educationalist David Holbrook, who in 1973 produced a swingeing attack, which ended thus:

> Most children probably read the stories as spooky yarns, and probably little harm is done. But under cover of his apparent religious intentions and his mask of benignity C.S. Lewis conveys to his readers a powerful unconscious message: that the world is full of malignancy . . . that aggression is glorious, exciting and fully justified; that tenderness, cowardice and reticence are weak; *that one may easily be assured of one's righteousness* (my italics); . . . and these messages are sometimes conveyed with undertones of a sadistic-sexual kind, or with powerful phantasies rooted in hate. This must surely raise doubts as to the wisdom of exposing children to them, from a writer of such clarity, persuasiveness and power.

Leaving aside the contradiction of the first and last sentences – either he does or doesn't have a potential effect – the essence of the problem surely lies in the italicised line: as Rowan Williams suggested, nobody is perfect, and one person's sadism is another person's heroism. But, as with politicians, it is the idea of being preached at by the self-righteous that seems to enrage many critics.

A linked problem is that often Lewis's personal prejudices blur into his religious views, and produce a kind of Christianity with which even believers are unsympathetic.

Sometimes his views are so transparent as to be risible, as at the beginning of *The Voyage of the Dawn Treader*:

> There was a boy called Eustace Clarence Scrubb, and he almost deserved it. . . . He didn't call his Father and Mother 'Father'

and 'Mother', but Harold and Alberta. They were very up-to-date and advanced people. They were vegetarians, non-smokers and teetotallers and wore a special kind of underclothes. In their houses there was very little furniture and very few clothes on the beds and the widows were always open.

Often his prejudices may be seen as more sinister, as at the end of *The Silver Chair* when Aslan, Jill, Eustace, and Caspian clear the bullies out of the playground:

> And then the Head (who was, by the way, a woman) came running out to see what was happening. . . . and she had hysterics and went back to the house and began ringing up the police. . . . After that, the Head's friends saw that the Head was no use as a Head, so they got her made an Inspector to interfere with other Heads. And when they found she wasn't much good even at that, they got her into Parliament where she lived happily ever after.

Well, what is wrong with a harmless side-swipe at politicians? Nothing, perhaps, but let us just go back to those parentheses. John Goldthwaite, an American critic who disliked Lewis and spent some time expounding this dislike in *The Natural History of Make-Believe* (1996), commented:

> I doubt there exists anywhere in children's literature a more dishonest parenthetical remark than this, or a more supercilious use of the phrase 'by the way'. . . . To assess how truly malicious an aside it is, substitute for 'woman' the word 'Jew' or 'Negro'.

And things might seem to be worse when Lewis parades his personal prejudices as religious dogma. In *Prince Caspian* there is another purging of a school:

> [Miss Prizzle] saw the lion, screamed and fled, and with her fled her class, who were mostly dumpy, prim little girls with fat legs. Gwendolen hesitated.
> 'You'll stay with us, sweetheart?' said Aslan.
> 'Oh, *may* I? Thank you, thank you,' said Gwendolen.

John Goldthwaite's view that this 'may well be the vilest passage ever to poison a children's book' may be something of an overstatement – there is, after all, a lot of competition. Nor is his view that the 'extraordinary assumption behind this passage is that there are no girls with fat legs among Lewis's readership – or else, perhaps, that their feelings are too inconsequential to matter' necessarily valid or there would be millions of unhappy girls with the wrong hairstyles upset by Enid Blyton. However, this is not just goodies versus baddies – it is Aslan/Christ gathering the elect, and that is a different matter. As Goldthwaite puts it,

> somewhere among the world's vast population of dumpy people with fat legs, there is one crestfallen schoolgirl who understands all too well the message of saintly Jack. . . . In the care of Saint Jack, the Last Judgement has become a beauty contest: no Prizzles allowed at that heavenly pub, the Lion and the Lamb, and no freckles and dumpies either. . . . People commonly, and unnecessarily, I think, worry about violence in some children's books. Here is the real violence.

Strong stuff, and Goldthwaite has not been alone. A.S. Byatt thought the books to be 'religious arm-twisting'. Philip Pullman went further, calling them 'wicked': 'I find them very dodgy and unpleasant – dodgy in the dishonest rhetoric way – and unpleasant because they seem to embody a world view that takes for granted things like racism, misogyny and a profound cultural conservatism that is utterly unexamined.' Perhaps another mystery is *why* this has been unexamined: are all readers, both adult and child, of Lewis's books, so unperceptive – or don't they think it matters, or don't they care?

The most obvious mystery here is quite why the attacks on Lewis are so visceral; Enid Blyton has been lambasted thoroughly but never with the kind of loathing expressed for Lewis by Goldthwaite and his ilk. Also – why has it become so personal? Enid Blyton's well-known shortcomings as a mother have been treated with a kind of solemn regret; Lewis provokes a character-assassinating biography from A.N. Wilson (described by one reviewer as 'a remarkable combination of superior writing and inferior judgement'). (It was Wilson who pointed out that the biopic *Shadowlands* distorted matters, not least because 'Anthony Hopkins, a brilliant actor, is immaculately clad in a dark suit, while Lewis was a filthy old man dripping beer and tobacco everywhere.')

And there are two other mysteries. The first is why it took so long for children's books critics to realise (and some have not yet done so) that Lewis's dictum 'I am almost inclined to set it up as a canon that a children's story which is enjoyed only by children is a bad children's story' is profoundly anti-child. It describes an underlying attitude of superiority, is fundamentally disrespectful of his audience – and it is one negative key by which we might unlock all the books. But there is also a religious mystery. In the words of Rowan Williams:

> Ultimately, the imagery of the wardrobe and the stable, standing at the beginning and the conclusion of the Narnia stories like bookends, is there to say something substantial about the whole relation of God to the world, the human Jesus to the divine Word, the body to the soul, the inexhaustible character of human identity itself.

Either way, the Narnia series remains the pivot of a debate that can only be healthy for the understanding of the importance and complexity of children's books.

21.

What Happened Next?
The Problem of Sequels

Whatever happened to the bar of silver left behind on Treasure Island? Did Mary Lennox grow up to marry Colin in *The Secret Garden*? Will Susan ever return to Narnia? Will Jo March become a successful writer? Many readers have speculated about such questions about their favourite stories. There is a natural curiosity to discover not only about the development of characters, but also about the solutions to problems or unfinished business that have been left unresolved at the end of a story.

Many authors answer these questions by carrying the story forward in a sequel themselves. Louisa M. Alcott (1832-88) showed in particular how such characters as Jo and Amy March developed in the three books that followed *Little Women*. Mary Norton's series about *The Borrowers* (1952), her tales about a little family living under the floors of an old country house, continued their adventures in *The Borrowers Afield* (1955), *The Borrowers Afloat* (1959), *The Borrowers Aloft* (1961), and *The Borrowers Avenged* in 1982. One of the most striking features of this series is the way Arietty, the young daughter of Pod and Homily, grows and matures into a fiercely stubborn but attractive independence. In more recent years J.K. Rowling, in her seven-volume series about her young hero, Harry Potter, from *Harry Potter and the Philosopher's Stone* in 1997 to *Harry Potters and the Deathly Hallows* in 2007, with brilliant invention and wit, covers the seven years Harry spent as a pupil at Hogwarts School of Witchcraft and Wizardry, to his final victory over the forces of evil embodied in the satanic figure of Voldemort.

Many sequels, especially those by individual authors, often portray actions and characters stretching over a period of time, and, as well as

21. What Happened Next? The Problem of Sequels

King of the sequels:
from Samuel Goodrich's *The Tales of Peter Parley About America* (1828).

showing a series of incidents, also depict the progress of the characters, not only physically from being a young new pupil to the sixth-former, but also tracing his or her moral and intellectual growth. But many series about a group of characters are much more free-standing and independent of other books in the series. In these stories time often seems to stand still and there is little change or development of character. Christopher Jennings, for example, the young hero of many books about him by Anthony Buckeridge, hardly changes from the first book in 1950 to the last in 1994.

The stories about William Brown, the young hero of Richmal Crompton's William books also show very few changes. Beginning with *Just – William* in 1922, Crompton produced thirty-eight books about William, ending with her posthumous *William the Lawless* in 1970. Although she made some effort to record changes in society over that period with references to pop singers and interplanetary travel in the later books, the familiar milieu of a suburban family remained largely unaltered, with the focus still upon William (aged eleven), and his gang of Ginger, Henry, Douglas, and the lisping but ever-threatening six-year-old Violet Elizabeth Bott. There is little character development there, although one notices that by the 1960s, Mrs Brown, who in the 1920s employed resident cook, housemaid, and gardener, is now reduced to a part-time cleaning lady.

The idea for a series of books about the same character or group of characters had long been popular. Perhaps because of the success of J. Fenimore Cooper's *Leatherstocking* adult novels about Natty Bumpo, the pioneering adventurer-hero of such tales as *The Last of the Mohicans* (1826), American publishers had successfully marketed series under a single name, such as Samuel Goodrich's numerous books under the pseudonym of Peter Parley, beginning with *The Tales of Peter Parley about America* in 1828. Although these were works of non-fiction, they probably pointed the way for Joseph Abbott (1803-79), who began a series of twenty-eight books about the adventures of twelve-year-old Rollo in 1836. Many of these early books were largely educational and instructive, but the idea of a series about the same character caught on with the American publisher Edward Stratemeyer (1862-1930). With the help of numerous ghost writers and pseudonyms, Stratemeyer built up a syndicate that in the early years of the twentieth century virtually mass-produced series of books for teenagers about such characters as the Bobbsey Twins, the Hardy Boys, and the mystery-solving young heroine, Nancy Drew. These formulaic and easy-to-read stories sold in their millions.

Often the energy behind a successful story, especially if it leaves unanswered questions, has led other writers to add to or to complete a work. One of the most successful of these is *St. Ives: Being the Adventure of a*

French Prisoner of War in England by Robert Louis Stevenson. Stevenson died unexpectedly in early middle age, leaving his adventure story unfinished, but he had outlined the rest of the story to Mrs Strong, his step-daughter and amanuensis, and she passed this information on to the well-known novelist Arthur Quiller-Couch and he successfully produced the last six chapters of Stevenson's work.

Many writers have been so stimulated by their reading that they have been inspired to write sequels to well-known works by other authors. *Treasure Island*, in particular, seems to have attracted writers, with such books as *The Adventures of Ben Gunn* (1956) by R.F. Delderfield (1912-1972), *Flint Island* (1972) by Leonard Wibberley, *Silver's Revenge: A Sequel to Treasure Island* (1979) by Robert Leeson (1928-2013), and most recently *Silver: Return to Treasure Island* (2012) by Andrew Motion (b. 1952).

What is interesting about many of these sequels is the way the authors sometimes take on a different perspective on a book's subject-matter from its original writer. William Horwood's sequels to Kenneth Grahame's *The Wind in the Willows* (1908), such as *The Willows in Winter* (1993), continues the adventures of that great anti-hero Toad of Toad Hall. But more radically, Jan Needle's book *Wild Wood* of 1981 portrays the stoats and weasels, the villains of Grahame's book, in a state of proper rebellion against the selfishness of Toad and the other river-dwellers. More recently in *Five Children on the Western Front* (2014), Kate Saunders takes up E. Nesbit's Edwardian fantasies in *Five Children and It* (1902) and *The Story of the Amulet* (1906) with its characters, as she saw them, 'eternal children, frozen for all time in a golden Edwardian summer'. But she realised that two of Nesbit's characters, Cyril and Robert, were a few years too old to be exactly the right age to end up being killed in the trenches of the Great War of 1914-18. *Five Children on the Western Front* opens in 1915 with the (now) older children still having amusing adventures with the grumpy Psammead or Sand Fairy, but, as they grow up, inevitably they become involved in the war. It is a memorable and poignant sequel.

The problem authors find in first creating and then continuing a series is, of course, the question of consistency. In producing a narrative involving numerous characters and events, spread over several books and a period of time, it is easy to forget the colour of the heroine's eyes or the names of minor characters. Usually the author's editor spots these kinds of slips, although no one seems to have noticed that Ginger Hebblethwaite, Biggles' young companion on many of his flying adventures, was surnamed Habblethwaite when he first appeared. Dates, too, can be overlooked, as well as ages, and while John Christopher Timothy Jennings remains somewhere between ten and eleven in all his years at Linbury Court School, in twenty-four books produced from 1950-1994, his great friend Darbishire's age fluctuates from twelve in *Our Friend Jennings* (1955) to eleven in *Especially Jennings* in 1965.

Some inconsistencies may be deliberate, of course. Malcolm Saville (1901-82) was the author of a series of adventures stories that ran from 1943 to 1978, about a group of children who call themselves 'The Lone Pine Club'. But over the series some children grow older, such as David, the leader of the group, who first appears as a fourteen- or fifteen-year-old public schoolboy, and subsequently becomes a solicitor in London; and in *Home to Witchend* (1978), the twentieth and final book in the series, David gets engaged to Petronella, another member of the club. Dickie and Mary, however, who are identical twins aged between nine and twelve, participate in all twenty adventures, but never grow up at all! Saville was well aware of the anomaly and explained that he deliberately wanted to strike a happy medium in his books, by allowing the older children to grow up, while the younger ones kept the childhood naivete, which had proved so entertaining to his readers.

Not surprisingly, the apparently unchanging world of the Just William stories that stretched over thirty-eight books from 1922 to 1970 contains many anomalies, too. William's friend Ginger is sometimes given the surname of Flowerdew and sometimes Merridew; Joan, the girl next door, is variously named Clive, Crew, or Parfitt; William's brother, Robert, is given the age of seventeen, eighteen, and nineteen, while his sister, Ethel, is always aged nineteen; William sometimes attends a boys' school and sometimes a co-educational establishment. One of the most startling slips concerns the treatment of William's dog, Jumble. He appears as William's companion in a completely matter-of-fact way in chapter 7 of *Just – William*, where they go off to a Band of Hope meeting, and later in the story Jumble devours William's pet rat, Cromwell! But in the final chapter of the book, William, while out for a walk, comes across a stray dog with a collar naming him as 'Jumble', which he adopts. Later in the chapter, however, Mr Jarrow, the real owner appears. He is a painter who is suffering from an artistic block, and he is so grateful to William for accidentally helping him to start painting again that he insists on presenting Jumble to him as a present, much to Mr Brown's dismay. This whole episode is related without any reference to the fact that William had already owned Jumble much earlier in the book. What has happened? Mary Cadogan, Richmal Crompton's biographer, suggests that, as most of the William stories first appeared as short stories in magazines, the publisher of the book was simply careless about placing the stories in the correct order when he collected them together for the book.

Although irritating at times, such anomalies or contradictions seem quite minor and trivial when compared with those works in which there appears to be a major dislocation between a book's original direction and quality, and a sequel that seems to contradict the true spirit of that which went before.

The *Flambards* trilogy by K.M. Peyton (b. 1929), for example, begins with *Flambards* in 1967, continues with *The Edge of the Cloud* (1969), which deservedly won the Carnegie Medal as best children's book of the year, and concluded with *Flambards in Summer* (1969). It gives a moving picture of adolescents moving towards maturity and love within the wonderfully realised context of Edwardian England and the Great War. But a later addition to the series, *Flambards Divided* of 1981, dismayed many readers because the direction of its narrative seemed to forget and almost repudiate the less class-based and more democratic values of the earlier books.

Both Louisa M. Alcott (1832-88) and Mark Twain (1835-1910) disappointed enthusiasts for their earlier works with rather lame continuations. *Little Women* (1868) and *Good Wives* (1869) develop the story of the March family with insight and warmth, but the later books, particularly *Jo's Boys* of 1886, which is about the fortunes of some of the boy-pupils from the school founded by Jo, read rather flatly like brisk summaries, and reveal Alcott's genuine reluctance to continue the series.

The stories of Mark Twain end in an even more dispiriting fashion. The brilliant humour found in *The Adventures of Tom Sawyer* (1876) and the richer insights of *The Adventures of Huckleberry Finn* (1884) were followed much later by the contrived and almost humourless tales of *Tom Sawyer Abroad* of 1894 and *Tom Sawyer Detective* of 1896. Mark Twain's later years were marked by serious family and financial problems – at one stage he even went bankrupt – and this might help to explain the sadness the reader feels on approaching these disappointing works.

The idea of sequels continue to fascinate both readers and writers. But the results may not always be satisfying. Conan Doyle, you may remember, brought Sherlock Holmes back to life in 1903 ten years after his apparent fall to his death at the Reichenbach Falls in 'The Final Problem', but as somebody once said, 'He was never the same man again.'

22.

To See Ourselves ...
What Image of the British
Do Children's Books Give the World?

This is one of the unfathomable mysteries – but it is far from being a trivial one.

Children's books are as important in creating or reinforcing images and ideas of national and international stereotypes as anything else. How we subconsciously feel about a nation may influence whether we like them or fight them, and it is clear that the subconscious attitudes imbued in us as children influence how we think as adults.

So we might begin by looking at what we, the British, think of other nations because of what we have learned to think as children by reading other nations' children's books. Then we might speculate on what *they* think of us. Of course, dear reader, should you not be British, you may well have your own answer. The difficulty of finding somewhere intelligent to stand on this issue is shown by extrapolating our narrow view of, say, French culture, to the French view of German culture or Japan's of Korea, or Brazil's of Argentina, and so on practically ad infinitum – given that most developed countries have huge outputs of children's books that are invisible to us.

The British – indeed, the Anglophone – myopia on this issue is reflected in the fact that the percentage of children's books translated into English bumps along year after year at around 2 per cent of the total published, whereas translations from English are, in several countries, more than 50 per cent of the total. As the otherwise shrewd commentator on children's literature, Alison Lurie wrote in a weak moment, 'Other nations have produced a single brilliant classic. . . . A list of famous children's books in

22. To See Ourselves

The quintessential image of the British?
John Tenniel's picture of Alice playing croquet in Lewis Carroll's
Alice's Adventures in Wonderland (1865).

English, however, could easily take up a page.' In a sense she is right, in that English texts have travelled the world, but Portuguese classics have only travelled the Portuguese world and Spanish classics have only travelled the Spanish world. On the other hand, Japanese (or Japanese-style) *Manga* comics swamp the British market, and for many, provide an enduring image of Japanese culture.

The question of why any book in any country becomes famous internationally is another question. For the most famous – *Pinocchio*, *Pippi Longstocking*, *Tom Sawyer* – it seems to have been a long and spontaneous process. Others, such as the Harry Potter books, have been marketed ruthlessly – or, if you prefer, with superb professionalism. The Harry Potter Experience at the Warner Brothers studios at Leavesden near London had at its peak 6,000 visitors a day – a high proportion from outside Britain. Hogwarts school, with its essentially class-based structures might well be the image of England that has travelled best – even so, what can a class-based private school mean to a (self-declared) classless society like Italy, or to a country that has no private schools? Presumably, it becomes another part of the fantasy, very remote from the British, or English, self-image – but what, then, are the implications for Britain in the world?

Perhaps the best-known books that are known throughout the world have been transmitted through the films of Walt Disney – and the process is accelerating through network television and other media. Disney has been much maligned (and generally unfairly) by cultural purists – to 'Disneyfy' has come to mean simplification and vulgarisation. But the Disney studios do not 'localise' the stories they begin with – as many books are 'localised' when they are translated – rather 'glocalised', that is, made globally accessible (or, perhaps, made into tool of American cultural colonisation). Disney demonstrates that although some texts are known all over the world, there can be no genuine international text, because the original has to be changed in both verbal and visual translation. In the case of a 'global' brand like Disney, the original story has, as it were, to be interpreted twice – once by the producers and directors into their concept of a global culture, and then that interpretation has to be reinterpreted by watchers or readers in individual countries.

And so, what do we think of other nations from their children's books?

Take, for example, France. The English image of France may be (depending on the generation that is observing) an amalgam of wine and baguettes, the *Tour Eiffel*, Charles de Gaulle, Audrey Tatou, various versions of Simenon's Maigret – and, as a sub-structure to all that, children's books. *Babar the Elephant*, *Ernest and Celestine*, *Asterix the Gaul*, and *Anatole* the mouse (written by an American, Eve Titus):

22. To See Ourselves

> In all France, there was no happier, more contented mouse,
>   than Anatole.
> He lived in a small mouse village
> near Paris
> with his dear wife DOUCETTE
> and their six children PAUL and PAULETTE, CLAUDE and
>   CLAUDETTE, GEORGES and GEORGETTE.

Then there is *Madeline* (written by an Austrian, Ludwig Bemelmans). Who, of a certain generation, does not see Paris as crocodiles of little girls passing pavement tables with the Eiffel Tower in the background?

> In an old house in Paris that was covered in vines
> lived twelve little girls in two straight lines.
> In two straight lines they broke their bread
> and brushed their teeth
> and went to bed.

France is a charming, whimsical place, with tree-lined boulevards, populated (if you have read the Ernest and Celestine books) by amiable bears in berets and chic mouse gamines.

Germany, to a certain generation, is *Emil and the Detectives* and perhaps Michael Ende's *The Neverending Story*; or perhaps it is the Brothers' Grimm, with dark forests and black bread. On the other hand, the German origins of *Struwwelpeter* have probably been forgotten, and English readers have certainly read it as a dark satire on the cautionary tale, while German readers might have taken it as representing *Kinderfeindlichkeit*, a cultural hostility to childhood.

Switzerland is Johanna Spyri's *Heidi* (*Heidis Lehr- und Wanderjahre* [1880]) – all cowbells and Alpine flowers and therapy with Clara, the disabled girl, brought back to health by the countryside:

> There was not one cloud in the deep blue sky. The great snowfield sparkled, and the massive bare peaks stood out clearly against the unbroken blue. The two girls sat side by side, as happy and contented as could be. From time to time one of the goats came and lay down beside them. Presently, Heidi thought of the meadow where all the flowers grew. . . . the yellow carpet of rock-roses, and the blue gleam of harebells, the sweet-scented primulas, and dozens of other flowers.

And how do we see the USA? There is quite a choice, although Mark Twain's *Adventures of Tom Sawyer* and Laura Ingalls Wilder's 'Little House on the Prairie' sequence from *Little House in the Big Woods* (1932) onwards might be good candidates.

The 'bad boy' tradition was never as strong in Britain as it was in the USA (William Brown is a late example), and so the image of the rebellious boy with bare feet and a fishing rod, pushing the boundaries of polite society and heading westward has been particularly potent. As Huck says at the end of *The Adventures of Huckleberry Finn*, the sequel to *Tom Sawyer*: 'But I reckon I got to light out for the Territory ahead of the rest, because Aunt Sally she's going to adopt me and sivilize me, and I can't stand it. I been there before.'

Wilder's account of Laura's travels in the pioneering era carries the same image: Pa Ingalls, remarkable as he was in real life, becomes the American superman. He can build anything, grow anything, play the fiddle, respect the Native Americans, and protect the environment – all without the help of, or despite the interference of, the government. As edited by Wilder's daughter, Rose, the story diverges somewhat from what actually happened (although the truth was dramatic enough) and emerges as a critique of Roosevelt's New Deal.

At the end of *Little House in the Big Woods*, Pa Ingalls goes out to shoot some game, but cannot bring himself to kill, successively, a deer, a bear, a doe, and a fawn, and comes home to the American idyll (where they can eat bread and butter instead):

> Laura lay awake a little while, listening to Pa's fiddle softly playing and to the lonely sound of the wind in the Big Woods. She looked at Pa sitting on the bench by the hearth, the firelight gleaming on his brown hair and glistening on the honey-brown fiddle. She looked at Ma, gently rocking and knitting.
>
> She thought to herself, 'This is now.'
>
> She was glad that the cosy house, and Pa and Ma and the firelight and the music were now. They could not be forgotten, she thought, because now is now. It can never be a long time ago.

It is clear that often translations – and marketing – may change books: Pippi Longstocking is read in Sweden as a critique of society, whereas in translation into English it is the broad comedy that is emphasised. Similarly, the books in Tove Jansson's 'Moomin' series (1945-70) are more whimsical than philosophical in translation (and on television). *Moominland Winter* (1958) in which Moomintrol wakes too early from his hibernation, demonstrates Jansson's serious touch. When spring really comes, a kind of lyrical nature-mysticism takes over:

22. To See Ourselves

The typical Italian?
An illustration by Enrico Mazzanti for the first edition of
Carlo Collodi's *Le avventure di Pinocchio* (1883).

The Snork Maiden had come across the first brave nose-tip of a crocus. It was pushing through the warm spot under the south window, but wasn't even green yet.

'Let's put a glass over it,' said the Snork Maiden, 'It'll be better off in the night if there's a frost.'

'No, don't do that,' said Moomintroll. 'Let it fight it out. I believe it's going to do still better if things aren't so easy.'

Suddenly he felt so happy that he had to be alone. He strolled off towards the woodshed.

And when nobody could see him any longer he broke into a run. He ran through the melting snow, with the sun warming his back. He ran simply because he was happy, with nothing at all to think about.

One curious thing about many of these books is that at first sight it might seem that they are too local – too bound to their specific time and place – to make a lasting impression around the world, let alone colour one country's view of another. Perhaps the most interesting case study is *Pinocchio*. Of Italy's two most famous children's books, one, De Amici's *Cuore*, translated as *Heart – An Italian Schoolboy's Journal*, is little known outside Italy. The other, which has become one of the most translated books in the world is Carlo Collodi's *Le Avventure di Pinocchio: Storia di un Burattino* (1883). Why the first, belonging to a genre recognisable worldwide, has failed to travel, while the other, deeply rooted in the political issues of the day, has, remains problematic. Even stranger is that the national image that Pinocchio embodies – wild, unreliable, erratic, and yet energetic and loyal – has not only been accepted by the world, but by Italians themselves. It is a paradoxical truth that nations seem to happily accept the image that their children's authors give them – even when, taken in the abstract, that image is not necessarily flattering. The Americans are backwoodsmen, the French are laid-back, the Italians passionate – but what of the English? What image do we give to the world?

Possibly the best-known British children's books, nationally and internationally, are the Alice books, *Mary Poppins*, *Peter Pan*, *Winnie-the-Pooh*, and *The Wind in the Willows*, all of which have caused Disney problems in different ways, possibly because Britishness stubbornly resists globalisation.

The most translated is undoubtedly *Alice*. In one of the most formidable scholarly research projects in the history of children's literature, *Alice in a World of Wonderlands*, there are essays by 251 writers on translations of the Alice books into 174 languages, among them Welsh *Anturiaethau Alys yng Ngwlad Hud*, Icelandic *Lísa í Undralandi*, and the language of Australian native peoples, Pitjantjatjara *Alitjinja ngura tjukurtjarangka – Alitji in the Dreamtime*. It is impossible to imagine what happens to translations into languages that, for example, have no puns, or what is lost if the Mad Hatter wears a fez rather than a top hat. Some indication of the problem might be the 1962 Italian version, *La Meravigliosa Alice*, which was subtitled *Una Lucida Invenzione, la Creazione Poetica di una 'Lolita' Vittoriana*. But for all that, the image that Alice might give to the world is more or less the opposite of Pinocchio: she is cool, unemotional, self-confident, even arrogant. Is this what it is to be quintessentially British – and is this perhaps how the world sees us?

If so, it is curious and worrying. Do we wish to be eccentric and bucolic, locked into our rituals of afternoon tea in an eternal Edwardian empire?

22. To See Ourselves

Or, possibly, some combination of eternal narrative truths and local flavour is the magic formula. Take our other international export, Beatrix Potter.

I have on my desk a beautifully produced edition of Beatrix Potter's *As Aventuras de Pedro Coelho*, and, as far as my grasp of Brazilian Portuguese goes, it is faithful to both the spirit and the letter of the original. But it has been somewhat localised. *A História de Pedro Coelho* begins:

> Era uma vez quatro coelhinhos. Eles se chamavam:
> Flocos,
> Flux,
> Rabo de Algodão
> e Pedro.
> Vivam com a mãe num banco de areia, debaixo das raízes de uma enorme figueira.
> Certa manhã, a velha sra. Josefina Coelho alertou:
> – Bem, meus queridos, vocês podem passear pelos campos ou dar uma volta na estrada, mas não entrem na horta do sr. Severino: o pai de vocês sofreu um acidente lá. A sra. Severina o transformou em recheio torta.

(Incidentally, and to my mind, delightfully, other Potter characters in this edition translate thus: Pati Pataxoca (Jemima Puddleduck), Porco Robinho, the Coelhinhos Felpudos, and the wicked Tommy Brock and Mr Tod, alias Tomé T. Xugo and sr. Raposao.

One can only, happily, assume that contemporary Brazilian children have the same robust sense of humour as British children of 1904, and recognise the sense of adventure, and the underlying edginess of the space in which the adventures take place, a space that Peter Rabbit shares with Tom Sawyer, Pinocchio, and the world. Even if they carry with them through life the idea that the British always have *leite e amoras* for tea, perhaps that is no bad thing.

23.

Why Is there no such Thing as Children's Poetry?
Ted Hughes and Michael Rosen

This may look like a hallucinatory question. A stroll around a children's bookshop, or most respectable bookshops with a children's section, will reveal a selection of brightly presented books of verse – and one might hazard a guess that the proportion children's poetry books to children's novels, and adult poetry to adult novels must be much the same. The difference is, of course, that children almost *never* write the *published* poems themselves.

So the fact is that a remarkable number of people – and this includes poets – fundamentally do not believe that children's poetry exists: more than that they believe that it *cannot* and perhaps even *should not* exist. It is like children's literature, an oxymoron, a contradiction in terms.

The logic is simple. We generally assume that poetry (at least, post-romantic poetry) is thoughtful, sophisticated, skilled, philosophical, crafted with a subtle skill in the language – and concerned with sex and death and interior states. The readership is assumed to be one that can give such texts the readings they demand and deserve. Now, the general view of children is that they are NOT thoughtful, sophisticated, skilled, philosophical, able to appreciate verses crafted with a subtle skill in the language – and they are not concerned with sex and death and interior states. Therefore, children's poetry cannot exist.

But what, then, is in all those books of children's poetry? Well, not *real* poetry. Poetry, as Jan Mark observed, is for 'those who have arrived rather than those who are on the way'; in other words, to appreciate poetry you need to have read a lot of poems. As children, by definition, cannot understand poetry, it is pointless to try to write it for them. And as for children actually writing poetry themselves . . . Here is the verdict of the poet Vernon Scannell:

> I can't think that a child of under, say, fourteen could write a poem that could truly be called a poem. . . . I can cite alleged poems by children which contain absolutely none of the qualities I've mentioned: craftsmanship, form, thought, apprehension of reality.

What adults can do, though, is to write something that resembles real, adult poetry; 'children's poetry' becomes a stepladder to, or training ground for, the real thing. So what most of those bright books contain (there are some noble exceptions) is some kind of lesser hybrid. As the poet (for adults) Roy Fuller pronounced, 'those who write poetry for children perforce enter the field of light verse'; or, as Dylan Thomas, more cheerfully put it in a list of how poets could make money: 'Children's poetry: this will kill you and the children.'

One strategy is to write 'what kids will like' – often a regrettably patronising idea. Consequently in the past there have been great quantities of what John Rowe Townsend called 'urchin verse' – based on the principle that 'kids like' rhythms and rhyme and jokes and have a short attention span (unlike, of course, most adults). There is still a lot of it about, but it is a rather sterile exercise, for as the children's poet Brian Morse said, 'Much [poetry] is produced for children nowadays . . . on the assumption that they need constant thrills. . . . But once you've had the quick laugh, where do you go from there?' A few years ago the situation had reached the point that, as Jan Mark observed, 'the look-kids-I'm-on-your-side rib-nudging . . . in the hands of some writers is beginning to look like child molesting'.

Often when we don't get merely the gag or the skit, we find an uneasy mixture of form and content. A.A. Milne, in an uncharacteristically casual moment, described the poems in *When We Were Very Young* (1924) thus: 'They are a curious collection; some *for* children, some *about* children, some by, with or from children', without apparently reflecting that this might have short-changed his young readers. We therefore have a poem with a joke for sharing with adults and children:

> What is the matter with Mary Jane?
> She's crying with all her might and main,
> And she won't eat her dinner – rice pudding again –
> What is the matter with Mary Jane?

A good many are about adults:

> I went down to the shouting sea,
> Taking Christopher down with me,
> For Nurse had given us sixpence each –
> And down we went to the beach.

And some for children that adults incidentally enjoy:

> John had
> Great big
> Waterproof
> Boots on . . .

The more inconsequential, perhaps, the better. When the poet John Drinkwater reviewed *When We Were Very Young* in *The Sunday Times* (those were the days) he distinguished between two voices in the book:

> 'the good Mr Milne' who writes verses for his son (like 'The King's Breakfast'), and the 'bad Mr Milne' who says 'If you are going to have a book of poetry, you must put some poetry into it' and who then produces 'Twinkletoes' or 'Water-lilies', with their pseudo-romantic 'fairy' images.

And he went on, very presciently, after admiring the 'child-centred' poems: 'It is all great larks, but I wonder whether the Sterner Critics will realise that [they are] also a very wholesome contribution to serious literature.' Whether adults can write children's poetry is questionable, but poetry written *without* one eye on educating its audience to like a certain form is at least a step on the way.

Of course, the motives for producing poetry books for children are not necessarily careless or commercial or malign, but, explicitly or not, they often support the stepping-stone theory of children's poetry. As Robert Bridges (Poet Laureate 1913-30) noted,

> There has been with regard to poetry a pestilent notion that the young should be gradually led up to excellence through lower degrees of it . . . and this has was carried so far that writers, who else make no poetical pretence, have good-naturedly composed poems for the young, and in a technique often as inept as their sentiment.

Therein lies the problem. If children's poetry is seen as a step (a low step) on a ladder to *real* poetry – that is, adult poetry, which has values and attributes that only adults can understand – then it is scarcely surprising that it will not be very good as far as adults are concerned and will be pretty well incomprehensible as far as children are concerned.

If that's what you want non-prose texts to be, then so be it – but what happens if we think the unthinkable, and look at what children themselves write? In a pure sense, children, who do not yet know 'the rules', produce their own (kind of) poetry. As Neil Philip, editor of the *New Oxford Book of Children's Poetry*, puts it: 'From the moment they can talk till the moment we finally convince them that what they have to say is not important, children are producing poetry the whole time.' Margaret Meek, a world expert on literacy – and not given to sentimentalising children – agrees: 'Children are natural poets, singing before they speak, metaphor-making before they prose their way to school.' School is there to impose rules on their natural creativity.

The tension between the adult desire to give children freedom, while at the same time inculcating the unexamined rules of poetic behaviour can be painful, as in Neil Philip's reluctant statement: 'But children can – and, with astonishing frequency do – make things out of language which, *if you can't strictly call them poems*, have more poetic intensity than most of what is written for them' (my italics).

This may seem to be an invitation to anarchy, and an abnegation of our educational responsibilities, but if we believe in 'children's poetry' rather than 'poetry for children', then we may be able to accept as valuable, as true poetry, something that doesn't look like anything we are used to. Children should be given the chance, as Alan Tucker put it, to 'build word castles and throw words around, more mess but more energy, light, and colour. Clearing up comes later.'

Compare Michael Rosen and Ted Hughes – both poets who encapsulate the problem. Rosen has the happy skill of being able to return to a childhood that contemporary children (and adults) recognise, and can empathise with. It is difficult to quote – Rosen is not the man for the *bon mot* (although his book titles, such as *Wait Until I'm Older than You* come close) – because Rosen is at his best as a narrative, performance poet. (To see examples, one can Google, for example, *Michael Rosen, No Breathing in Class*). This is poetry that is alive, that encourages engagement with words. For older audiences he can be refreshingly forthright:

> Welcome to the museum.
> First we'd like to show you round the dress collection.
> Here you can look at the clothes:

> Dresses, shoes, hats, coats and so on
> Worn for the last 400 years
> By rich shits.

Rosen's work crosses the no person's land between children's and adults' skills and perceptions – it is serious, sympathetic, and empathetic play. In some ways he is giving the voiceless a voice – and, as Terry Pratchett once observed, that is generally known as blasphemy.

But if Rosen might be dismissed as a mere entertainer (and how, one wonders, did that become a pejorative term?), then good 'children's poetry' is not necessarily produced by more revered poets. John Wain, selecting Ted Hughes as the first winner of the *Signal* Poetry Award, conceded that 'None of this is exactly poetry for children; have we, as selectors, simply yielded to the temptation to pick the book that seems to us to contain the best poems, as poems, and devil take the hindmost classroom teacher?'

That statement seems to me to encapsulate an 'adultist' attitude that can lead even the best writers into unfortunate places. In many ways, Ted Hughes, described by the Poetry Foundation as being 'unequivocally recognised as one of the greatest poets of the 20th century', epitomises the problem. In his (at the time) much-respected handbook of writing and teaching poetry, *Poetry in the Making* (1967), he took a poetic view of poetry that was sympathetic to the young poet:

> It is when we set out to find words for some seemingly quite simple experience that we begin to realise what a huge gap there is between our understanding of what happens around us and inside us, and the words we have at our command to say something about it. Words are tools, learned late and laboriously and easily forgotten. . . . They are unnatural, in a way, and far from being ideal for their job.

The problem in our present context is that in writing for children Hughes often seemed to lose touch with his own poetic standards. I don't just mean such collections of squibs such as *Meet My Folks* (1961) that the *TLS* described as 'Wonderfully fresh'. Fresh they may be, but competent verse they are not. A random example:

> Some fathers work at the office, others work at the store,
> Some operate great cranes and build up skyscrapers galore,
> Some work in canning factories counting green peas into cans,
> Some drive at night in huge and thundering removal vans.

It merely strikes me that if one is going to set out to write in a scanning, rhyming form, then one might make some effort to make the verses scan (the same is true of every verse in the collection) and not to force the rhymes by changing from British to American English at need. I would also worry about the self-evidently and self-consciously Serious and Dramatic poetry:

> The Sun's an iceberg
> In the sky.
> In solid freeze
> The fishes lie.
> Doomed is the Dab
> Death leans above –
> But the Heron
> Poised to stab
> Has turned to iron
> And cannot move.

Hughes made a reputation as an authentic nature-writer . . . but the dab (*Pleuronectes limanda*) is a sea fish, commonly living between six and 130 feet . . . which would need a very long-necked heron (especially as herons usually hunt in fresh water). Also, if the dab is already frozen, how can it be doomed? Is this supposed to rhyme and to be metrical – and if so what happens in the second half? And why the poetic inversion (why not 'the Dab is doomed'?) To an unsympathetic observer – that is, one sympathetic to children – it all looks to be rather careless and demeaning stuff. Of course, no poet should be condemned on the grounds of their worst work – we are all human, and, after all, what might be condemned is the continued publication of such questionable materials.

To sum up, then, genuine *children's* literature and *children's* poetry is precisely that which has no appeal to adults; thus children's poetry should not be seen as a bridge or a ladder to anything – except, perhaps, as part of an openness of mind to language and its possibilities. This is a paradoxical, challenging area. As Margaret Meek said, 'Part of the puzzle and the fun of poetry for the young is that it works contrary to what they are learning to do to be good at reading.' Michael Rosen makes a similar point:

> If you think for a moment, very nearly all children enter school, using a language that is theirs, only to find that school is full of language that seems to belong to other people. If poetry plays with language and, through its music, invites children to remember and imitate it, this becomes a language that they can possess.

But what on earth would this poetry look like? Perhaps a single example might suffice. Through the 1980s there was a series – *Cadbury's Book of Children's Poetry* – based on an annual competition for children. While, predictably, there was some 'unskilled' imitation of adult forms of poetry, there were many soaring examples of writers escaping from imposed order, such as the four-year-old Anna Burgess from *Cadbury's Ninth Book of Children's Poetry* (1991), with her poem 'Mummie's Skirt':

> Pick me up in your wonderful skirt
> All the day long!

Now that, it seems to me, is *real* children's poetry.

24.

Which Are the Best 100 Children's Books?

There's an old football joke. 'Which are the two best football teams in Manchester?' 'Why, that's easy,' says the Manchester United fan to his Manchester City rival, 'Manchester United and Manchester United Reserves.' The same kind of answer might be expected if you were to ask many ten-year-old children 'What are the best 100 children's books?' 'Why, that's easy,' he or she might say, 'the first hundred written by Enid Blyton.'

These thoughts are prompted by the recent publication by the Grolier Club in America entitled *One Hundred Books Famous in Children's Literature*. There have been numerous similar attempts in the past to select the most worthy books from as long ago as the *Juvenile Review* of 1817. But there are many difficulties in attempting such a venture. There is, for example, the problem of how to deal with prolific authors. The *Observer* newspaper recently produced a list entitled 'The Greatest English-language Novels of all Time', and beginning with *Pilgrim's Progress* of 1678 reached 100 with the *True History of the Kelly Gang* by Peter Carey, a work that was published in 2000. But it reached that number by limiting authors to a single work only. A list that did not have that restriction might have reached 100 simply by including more works by nineteenth-century novelists alone, if you counted all the works of such writers as Charles Dickens, Sir Walter Scott, and Anthony Trollope!

To be fair, the most recent attempt by the famous Grolier Club of America lists is the 2014 edition of *One Hundred Books Famous in Children's Literature*. Thus it deliberately evades the question of pronouncing on a book's literary quality by concentrating on its historical importance.

The range is certainly impressive, starting chronologically with the *Orbis Sensualis Pictus* of 1658, which is generally regarded as one of the most significant schoolbooks ever written, and reaching 100 with J.K. Rowling's publishing sensation *Harry Potter and the Philosopher's Stone* in 1997, taking in such works as Perrault's fairy tales (1697), *Struwwelpeter* (1845), *Alice's Adventures* (1865), and *The Wizard of Oz* (1902). Even if one's eyebrows are slightly raised by the presence in a work about children's literature of *Robinson Crusoe* (1719) and *Gulliver's Travels* (1726), and one is surprised by the absence of Mrs Sherwood, author of the notorious *History of the Fairchild Family* (1818-47), one can see what this list is about all right.

Other modern attempts by such authors as Kathleen Lines, Peter Hollindale, and the Book Trust, may be more problematic. Kathleen Lines was a distinguished librarian and publisher, who in 1950 produced the revised work *Four to Fourteen: A Library of Books for Children*. Aimed at parents and teachers and all those interested in children's reading, her wide-ranging and meticulously annotated selection included nursery rhymes, fairy tales, fiction, and a good deal of non-fiction, such as books about art and architecture and music. Peter Hollindale (b. 1936), a distinguished academic and critic of children's literature, made an equally judicious selection of books for children, giving reasons for his selection in *Choosing Books for Children* (1974).

Although Kathleen Lines made it clear that she did not intend to produce a list of the best books for children, more recent works have made bolder claims. Julia Eccleshare, for example, entitled her list *1001 Children's Books You Must Read Before You Grow Up* (2009). Her recommendations are organised for various age groups, such as zero to three, over eight, and over twelve, and the selection is wide-ranging, including translations of Chinese, Dutch, Italian, Japanese, and Russian stories. In 2015 the independent charity Booktrust was equally confident when it published its list of the best 100 children's books from the past 100 years. It's a catholic list, ranging from picture books for younger children, such as Anthony Browne's *Gorilla* (1983) and Eric Carle's *The Very Hungry Caterpillar* (1970) to more controversial fiction for adolescents, such as Judy Blume's *Forever* (1975) and *Junk* (1996) by Melvin Burgess. While it appears to ration the more prolific authors, such as Enid Blyton (1897-1968), to only two entries, it seems odd that it doesn't find space for John Masefield's *The Midnight Folk* (1927) or *The Box of Delights* (1935), or Russell Hoban's *The Mouse and his Child* (1967) or *How Tom Beat Captain Najork and his Hired Sportsmen* (1974).

There had been earlier attempts, of course. Mrs Sarah Trimmer (1741-1810) had used her, usually religious, criteria for recommending children's books in her Evangelical periodical *Guardian of Education* which appeared

24. Which Are the Best 100 Children's Books?

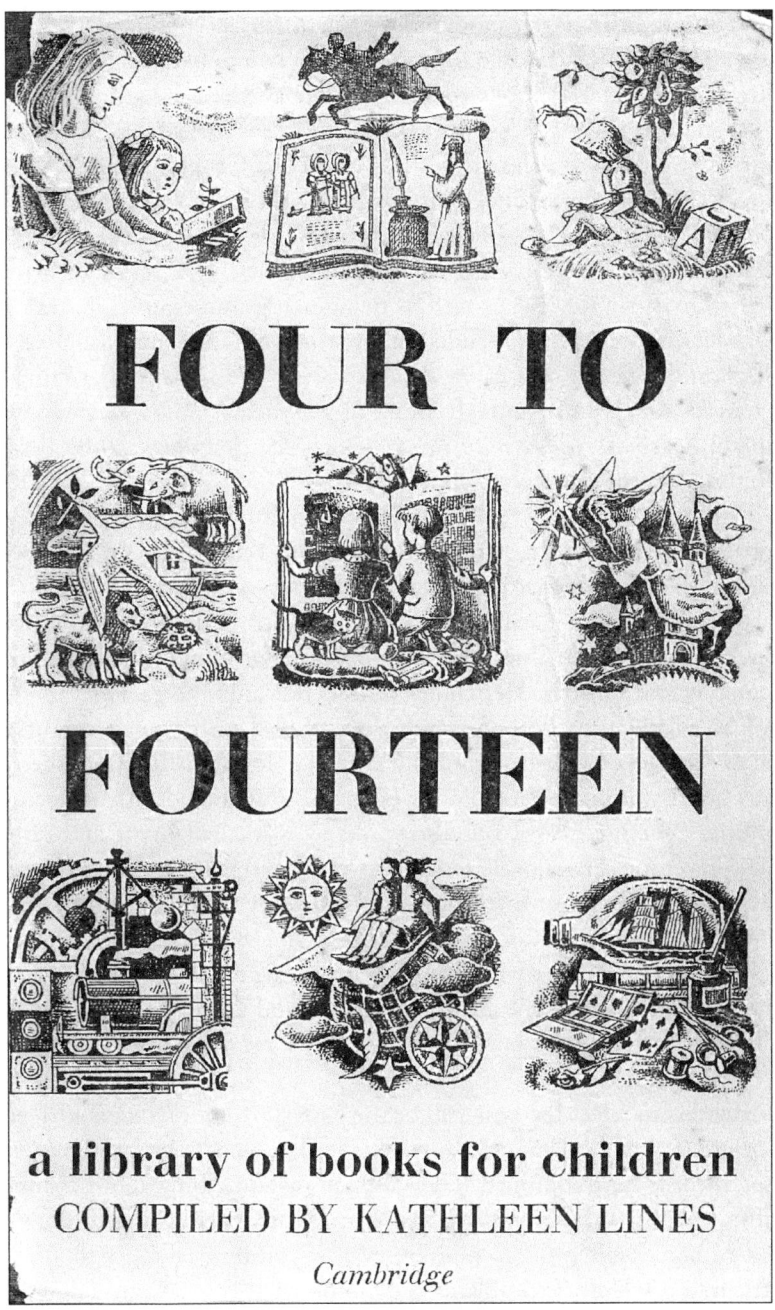

A distinguished booklist from the 1950s:
Kathleen Lines's *Four to Fourteen* – with an introduction by Walter de la Mare.

from 1802-6. In 1817 the anonymous *Juvenile Review* contained a selection of books suitable for children from the ages of two to five and five to eight, listing over a hundred books by such authors as Maria Edgeworth (1767-1849) and Isaac Watts (1674-1748). In the list of books for children aged eight to twelve, as well as suggesting works on Geography and Natural History, it also recommended stories by Maria Edgeworth and Barbara Hofland (1770-1844), as well as *The Swiss Family Robinson*. In 1844 Elizabeth Rigby (later Lady Eastlake [1809-93]), in a series of articles for the *Quarterly* Review, as well as denouncing numerous dull, didactic books for children, recommended many works for enjoyment, such as the collection of tales in *The Home Treasury* (from 1843), as well as fantasies such as *Undine* (1818), and adventure stories such as *Robinson Crusoe* and Captain Marryat's *Masterman Ready,* which she describes as 'the best of Robinson Crusoe's numerous descendants'.

Charlotte M. Yonge (1823-1901), herself a considerable novelist, probably made the most systematic nineteenth-century attempt to codify children's books in her work entitled *What Books to Lend and What to Give* of 1887. She gives a classified list of books suitable for children, ranging from books for 'Little Ones' and 'Senior Classes' to those on such topics as Biography and History. Her choice reflects not only the greater variety of books available for children towards the end of the nineteenth century, as well as the wider sympathies of adult critics as devout as Charlotte herself. Thus her list of books suitable for boys not only includes that perennial favourite *Robinson Crusoe*, but also works by R.M. Ballantyne and Robert Louis Stevenson. Her 'novelettes and novels' that she describes as 'fit for the growing maiden' not only include seven works by Charlotte Yonge herself but two novels by the more daring Mrs Gaskell (1810-65). Her list of fairy tales, works often bitterly condemned at the beginning of the century, as we have seen, include the Brothers Grimm and Hans Andersen, as well as Lewis Carroll's Alice books and *The Light Princess* (1864) by George MacDonald.

Attempts to select the best 100 or the best 1001 children's books reveal, of course, a good deal about history. They tell us what books were available when the lists were compiled. They also tells us something about changing cultural attitudes. But there are many problems when trying to draw up a list of books suitable for children, even if you limit authors to a single entry each. One of the problems is defining what is meant by a children's book. Is *Pilgrim's Progress*, that great religious allegory, really a children's book? And what about recommending other adult works, such as Swift's political satire *Gulliver's Travels*, simply because many children have read them? Attempting to list books for specific age groups present problems, too, because children differ. What is suitable and immensely enjoyed by some young children may fall flat with others of the same age range. Times change, too. What was apparently compulsive for a teenage girl in 1850 may seem absolutely tame fifty years later.

In the end, of course, selections and recommendations of good books depend upon the criteria used in the selection, whether they are the evangelical beliefs prevalent in the early nineteenth century or the more secular values of modern times. Making up such lists can be a harmless bit of fun, of course, rather like selecting one's ideal cricket team. ('Should W.G. Grace open the batting with Geoffrey Boycott, or should I pick Jack Hobbs?') But in the end the selector who wants to do well for children, by choosing books that are considered the 'best', tells us something about him or herself, revealing something of personal pleasures, hopes, and anxieties. As Russell Hoban (1925-2011), the author of so many brilliant books for children, says in *Turtle Diary* of 1975:

> People write books for children and other people write about the books written for children, but I don't think it's for the children at all. I think that all the people who worry so much about the children are really worrying about themselves, about keeping their world together and getting the children to help them do it, getting the children to agree that it is indeed a world. Each new generation of children has to be told: 'This is a world, this is what one does, one lives like this.' Maybe our constant fear is that a generation of children will come along and say: 'This is not a world, this is nothing, there's no way to live at all.'

25.

And Which Is *the* Best?

The Carnegie Medal and Other Awards

In 1936, the Library Association (since 2002, more grandly, the Chartered Institute of Library and Information Professionals [CILIP]) founded the Carnegie Medal (it was the centenary of the birth of the philanthropist Andrew Carnegie) – an award for 'an outstanding book for children published during the previous year'. Every year since then, except in 1943, 1945, and 1966, when no books were considered suitable, the decision has been queried somewhere. This is not really surprising: what does 'outstanding' mean?

In 1977, Alec Ellis, who had been a judge of the award, wrote, 'It cannot be emphasised too frequently that popularity is not a criterion for the award.' Which, for some readers, brings us to an immediate impasse. For if a children's book is not popular with children, then how can it be regarded as being outstanding? Children are not like adults, who are quite capable of awarding prizes to books that few people read – it has been estimated that only a tiny percentage of Man Booker winners bought are actually read – and for some years it became a byword of librarians that the Carnegie-winning books were the ones least likely to be borrowed from children's libraries.

So why not let the children judge, after all, since they are the readers; and the answer is that it is like saying let the patients prescribe their own drugs – after all, they have to swallow them. Adults have, so the argument goes, to judge children's books for them, not only because children aren't capable of judging, but because they *shouldn't* be allowed to judge anyway. Brian Alderson in a controversial article in 1969, 'The Irrelevance of Children to the Children's Book Reviewer', summed up this position:

25. And Which Is *the* Best?

> It may be objected that to assess children's books without reference to children is to direct some absolute critical standard relating neither to the author's purpose nor the reader's enjoyment. To do much less, however, is to follow a road that leads to a morass of contradictions and subjective responses.

That is, it leads to a loss of adult power, the power to prescribe what is good or bad. As Fred Inglis put it in his *The Promise of Happiness*, perhaps even more forcefully:

> Irrespective of what a child makes of an experience, the adult wants to judge it for himself, and so doing means judging it for *it*self. The judgement comes first, and is at least logically separable from doing the reckoning for children. *Tom's Midnight Garden* and *Puck of Pook's Hill* are wonderful books whoever you are, and that judgement stands whether or not your child can make head or tail of them.

Adults commission, write, and publish books, so theirs is the judgment. Little wonder that those outside the literary-critical bubble doubt whether the balance between critic and reader is quite right.

Ellis noted that some books seemed to have been published 'with the express purpose of receiving its accolade' of the Carnegie Medal – indeed, in its history it is easy to see *types* of books clustering together. Between 1954 and 1965, for example, Oxford University Press won the Medal eight times and had a large share of the shortlist. The Carnegie list is a kind of rollcall of classic children's books, but how could it be otherwise – the approved define what is to be approved: *Pigeon Post, The Borrowers, The Last Battle, Tom's Midnight Garden, The Owl Service, Watership Down, Northern Lights, Skellig* . . . No Roald Dahl or Enid Blyton – that is not what we are about.

Robert Westall was a case in point. His *The Machine Gunners* won the 1975 Carnegie, and, as he wrote in 1979, this changed his attitude:

> Crawlingly and contemptibly . . . I began writing books for the children of publishers, librarians, and the literary gent of *The Times*. . . . Now that I am at least conscious of what I was doing, I look round and see so many 'good' children's books written for the same bloody audience. Books that gain splendid reviews, win prizes, make reputations and are unreadable by a majority of children.

Today, it may well be that books are written to *challenge* the judges.

But to return to the idea of 'outstanding'. Back in the day, the day being in 1972 when academic debates about children's books were in their infancy, the Carnegie Medal went to one of K.M. Peyton's Flambards novels, *The Edge of the Cloud* – reissued in 2014 – the Downton Abbey of its day. One strong objection, from Dominic Hibberd, was that it was 'teenlit', and that the judges seemed to be using standards 'which in kind are the same as adult ones, but which in degree are lower and less demanding'. In short, this book wasn't 'literature'. One of the judges, the distinguished librarian Colin Ray replied,

> the award is for an 'outstanding' book. . . . I would personally criticise that adjective for being vague: but one thing it does not explicitly mean is that the Medal is a literary award. . . . In considering quality, literary quality is only one aspect: its potential impact on the young reader, its idea, its chances of being read, its individual aspects which make it stand out from the rest, all are relevant.

This is a fascinating debate because it shows critics and librarians trying to work out, on the hoof, as it were, precisely what standards and values they are applying to children's books: adult methods and values (whatever they were, and whether scaled down or not) did not seem to meet the case.

How have things developed in forty years? The criteria for awarding the Medal have, it seems, been considerably refined: here is an extract from the 2016 requirements of the CILIP, which begins, perhaps not very encouragingly: 'The book that wins the Carnegie Medal should be a book of outstanding literary quality.' Which, of course, gets us nowhere; indeed, it sets us back a little as it now has *two* difficult-to-define terms, 'outstanding' and 'literary'. But the criteria-masters, perhaps aware of this, try to pin things down a little:

> The whole work should provide pleasure, not merely from the surface enjoyment of a good read, but also the deeper subconscious satisfaction of having gone through a vicarious, but at the time of reading, a real experience that is retained afterwards.

Which might seem reasonable, although it might exclude, say, books about the holocaust, or the 2014 winner, *The Bunker Diary* (indeed, most of the recent winners) – unless you have a somewhat gloomy view of pleasure. And perhaps *all* books provide subconscious satisfaction – especially bestsellers such as Blyton or Dahl. In fact, that paragraph simply introduces five more arguable terms – 'pleasure', 'surface enjoyment', 'good read', 'a real experience', and 'retained afterwards'.

But, as is so often the case, people in a hole tend to keep digging. The advice goes on to list eighteen non-mandatory characteristics. Here is a selection, almost all of which make matters worse:

> Style:
> How successfully has the author created mood, and how appropriate is it to the theme?
> Do dialogue and narrative work effectively together?
> How effective is the author's use of literary techniques and conventions?
> How effective is the author's use of language in conveying setting, atmosphere, characters, action etc.?
> Characterisation:
> Are the characters believable and convincing?
> Do they act consistently in character throughout the book?
> How effectively are the characters revealed through narration, dialogue, action, inner dialogue and through the thoughts, reactions and responses of others?
> Are they well-rounded, and do they develop during the course of the book?
> The plot:
> Is it well-constructed?
> Does the author appear in control of the plot, making definite and positive decisions about the direction events take and the conclusions they reach?
> Do events happen, not necessarily logically, but acceptably within the limits set by the theme?

The only question that is actually objectively answerable is 'Where factual information is presented, is this accurate?' (and even that one spoils the effect by adding the unquantifiable qualification 'and clear'). Seeing as the last time the Carnegie was awarded to a non-fiction book was over sixty years ago – *A Valley Grows Up* by Edward Osmond – that criterion does not seem to be particularly important.

One is at a loss: the more the list tries to be objective, the less objective it becomes – we are left with a bunch of subjective judgements, some of them bewildering. For example, what is the difference between 'believable and convincing'?; if the author is not in control of the plot, who is?; characters must act consistently – no Hamlets or Earls of Dorincourt need apply; and no unrounded minor background characters can creep in.

It is, however, instructive to watch an attempt to backhandedly define the kind of book that is acceptable – and a pretty conservative kind of book it is. The Carnegie – although I am sure that this is not the intention – begins to look like a last-ditch stand against the forces of electronic and social media, with their utterly different concepts of narrative.

The Man Booker prize criterion for the winner is 'the best novel in the opinion of the judges': why is that simple formulation not good enough for a children's book award? The answer is that, perhaps to their credit, children's book awards are conflicted over what children should read, on all sorts of levels – what they might enjoy, what will be good for them, what is culturally acceptable, and so on. Adult book awards may be conflicted by demonstrating that the judges appreciate the kinds of books that they should be reading, for their own intellectual reputation, but that is not quite the same thing. No Man Booker judge, surely, feels *responsible* for their judgements.

But there are other children's book prizes: some are voted for only by children, notably the Children's Book Award of the Federation of Children's Book Groups, and, perhaps not surprisingly, they tend to present their prizes to non-Carnegie-winners such as J.K. Rowling and Anthony Horowitz. The Children's Book Award has a complex voting system based on 'testing' the books on children – books submitted and supplied by publishers – to avoid the inherent problem that children can only vote on what they've been given. Even with these safeguards, adults cannot avoid being in control.

The Whitbread Awards (from 2006 renamed the Costa Awards), were intended to be a little more downmarket – and are notable for the winner of the children's book section twice being named Book of the Year – Philip Pullman's *The Amber Spyglass* (2001) and Frances Hardinge's *The Lie Tree* (2015) – a level playing field at last! The awards were perhaps less distinguished for the unseemly arguments over the 1999 award when the bestselling *Harry Potter and the Prisoner of Azkaban* was beaten by the largely (one suspects) unread, *Beowulf*. But at least the award stayed true to its principles: 'the best [book] in the opinion of the judges'.

Fundamentally, children's book awards – like any other literary or artistic awards – cannot ever be more than arbitrary, but that does not mean that they are not influential, commercially important, or, indeed, prestigious. The Astrid Lindgren Memorial award is, at 5,000,000 Swedish Krona (£406,511 in 2019) one of the richest three or four literary prizes in the world (the Man Booker is said to be about the 40th). If nothing else, they reflect what the authorities in children's books would wish children's books to be, as well as what they actually are.

Yet, at the very least those who are judging Children's Book Awards tend to have some idea of their responsibility *in loco parentis*. There is also the possibility, at least, that the supposed innocence of childhood will have an influence on the judges. One would hope that the Carnegie is unlikely to receive the kind of criticism directed at the Booker: in 2001, A.L. Kennedy, who was a judge in 1996, called the prize 'a pile of crooked nonsense' with the winner determined by 'who knows who, who's sleeping with who, who's selling drugs to who, who's married to who, whose turn it is'. Not, surely, in children's book land.

26.

A Mystery Solved:
How Adults Read Children's Books

As you are reading this, you are probably a reader (if only occasionally) of children's books – and possibly an enthusiast for children's books in general, or for one genre or author – and you may well have encountered sceptics who wonder why you are reading books that are patently not for *us adults*. And as children are by definition inexperienced and unskilled readers, and books written for them (the argument goes) must be, by definition, inferior, are we admitting to inferiority, or are we soggy with nostalgia, or, worse, have we not grown up? Any way one looks at it, what we are doing is pretty suspect.

There are several ways of replying to this. One is C.S. Lewis's robust approach, which argued for liking things of childhood and things of adulthood: 'I now like hock, which I am sure I should not have liked as a child. But I still like lemon squash. I call this growth and development because I have been enriched; where I formerly had only one pleasure, I now have two.'

But there is no need for special pleading: it is simplest to point out that by reading – and enjoying – a children's book, you are not only giving the book a genuinely *literary* reading (serious, involved), but that you are doing something at least twice as difficult as when you read an adult book.

When you, as an adult, read a book written for adults, you are reading, at most, in two ways: primarily you are reading for *yourself* – for enjoyment, absorption, stimulation – and you will be accepting the book on its own terms. Secondarily, if you are a student, a member of a book-reading club, or have an attentive partner, you may be reading (simultaneously) analytically, in order to talk about or discuss the book.

26. A Mystery Solved

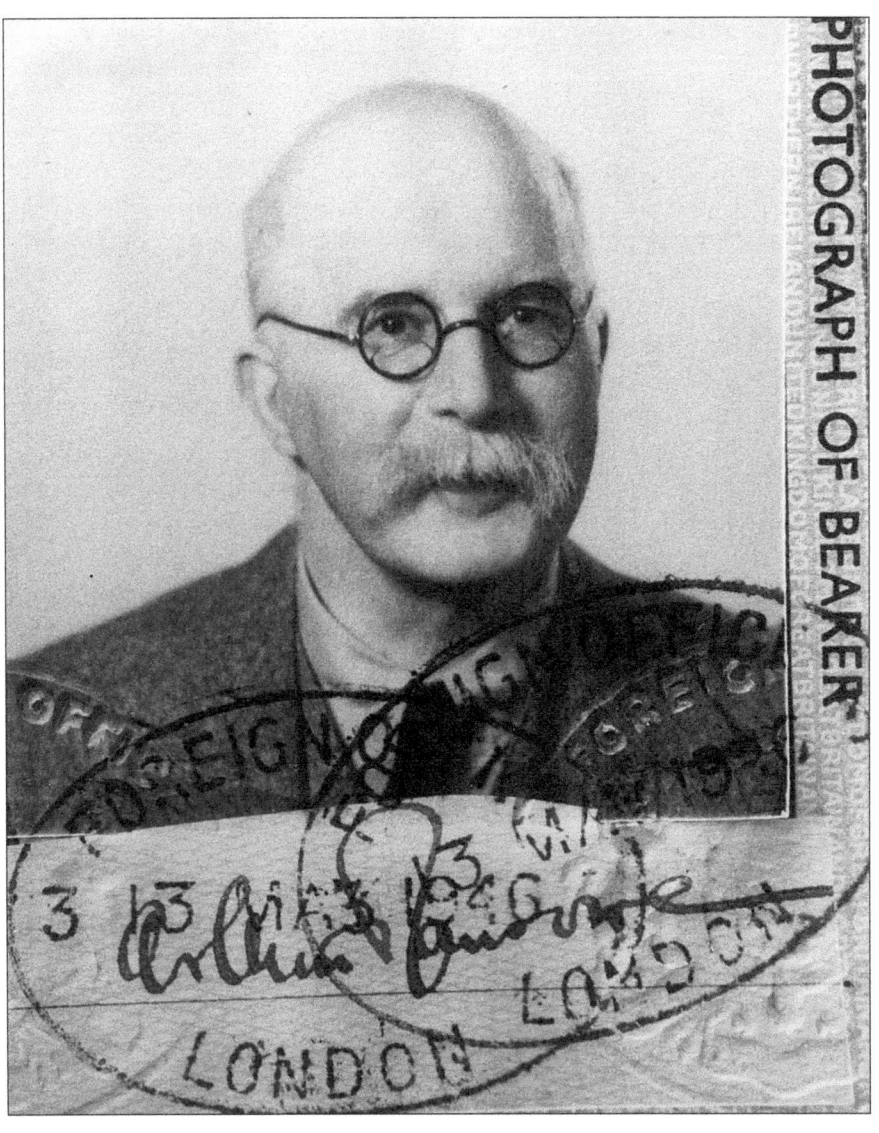

Passport to adventure:
Arthur Ransome (1884-1967).

In contrast, an adult reading a children's book will – necessarily, it's not an option – read in at least five ways. One may be dominant, but the others will be there in the background.

The first is the one that readers will either vehemently deny or vehemently agree that they are doing: this is to read for one's present, adult self, using adult perceptions and perhaps selecting those parts of the books that appeal to adult interests. This is reading the book on your own terms, not necessarily on the author's terms.

The second, if you are lucky, is the one that you will most often be doing – reading for your *inner* child *as* your inner child. You are, as it were, surrendering yourself to the book. You are becoming, or accepting the role of, the implied reader. (It is a long-standing literary theory that every book implies what its ideal reader should be like, should know, and appreciate – and whenever you pick up a book you subconsciously decide whether to be that reader.) This is the kind of reader that authors want.

But there is another child lurking in the psyche, the child that you *were*, however remote, however partial, however half-remembered. When you read for, or *as* this child, you are not simply indulging in nostalgia (if nostalgia can be seen as an indulgence): the reading is a combination of memory, perhaps visceral reactions. You are reading for your past, lost child – and, given the ambivalent relationship that most of us have with our childhood, it can be a painful process.

Fourthly, you are reading analytically, for your peers, to discuss what you are reading, and this will often overlap with the fifth way of reading – reading *on behalf of* the child. Children's books are, at root, about power and control, and it is natural for an adult who has any involvement in the process of linking book to child to consider whether a book is suitable (in the widest sense) for a specific child, or group of children – perhaps even for children in general – whether they will like it, whether they should be given it, or whether they should be protected from it.

That's the theory, but how does it look in practice?

I can thoroughly recommend trying a literary experiment. Choose a book, or an author's works, and ask yourself – what happens when you read? Which kind of reading produces which kind of response in yourself? It is a very introspective, personal process, not at all related to the grand simplifications of cultural demagogues and literary value-setters, but it is *real*; it is what happens when we read, and it is far from simple.

I can only demonstrate this with a personal example. I have chosen the Swallows and Amazons series by Arthur Ransome because there is at least a chance that the readers of this book might have some familiarity with that writer; I could have used another, or many other authors, but there might be even less chance of making my point. Personally, I came away from the experience with, I think, a better understanding of my relationship(s) with the books – and even of my relationship with my childhood – and a better understanding of how to answer those who think that adults reading children's books is a pretty profound mystery in itself.

1. Reading for My Adult Self

It may possibly be useful to know that I am an academic in my seventies who has been reading Ransome since about age seven (the earliest dated copy I can find in my collection is of *The Big Six* given to me in 1955 when I was ten – and I had been collecting the set for some time). Being a bookish child, at the age of eleven I produced a fold-out chart of the chronology – season by season – of the books; compounding this tendency, or felony, in 1991 I wrote a book-length introductory study of Ransome. I do not sail, or fish, or (willingly) camp out; I still dip into the books and sometimes listen to Gabriel Woolf's excellent audio adaptations.

Ransome's twelve Swallows and Amazons books, published between 1930 and 1947, were part of the 'camping and tramping' fashion of the period, and Ransome was instrumental in exploiting the combination of practically described outdoor activities, holidays, groups of semi-independent children, and more-or-less plausible incidents. *Swallows and Amazons*, set in 1929, brings the Walker children to the Lake District for their summer holidays, where they borrow a dinghy (*Swallow*) and camp on an island in the lake. They meet the local Blackett girls, whose dinghy is called *Amazon*, and they camp, sail, fish, and retrieve a stolen trunk. The following summer, they are reunited in *Swallowdale* (1931) for similar low-key 'adventures' – the Amazons have their activities limited by the presence of a disciplinarian Great Aunt. That winter, they are joined for *Winter Holiday* (1933) by Dick and Dorothea, who, in the following spring (fictional 1932) are on holiday on the Norfolk Broads. In *Coot Club* (1934) they meet a new group of children who are dedicated sailors, and whose hobby is protecting birds. When one bird is threatened by inconsiderate visitors, one of the children, Tom, casts off their hired cruiser. The rest of the book is concerned with the visitors pursuing the children around the Broads. That summer, Dick and Dorothea are back in the Lake District to join the Walkers and the Blacketts for *Pigeon Post* (1936), in which the children prospect for gold and are involved in a fell fire. That autumn takes Dick and Dorothea back to the Broads for a detective story, *The Big Six* (1940), in which three local boys are accused of casting off boats. In (fictional) 1933, the Walker children effectively grow up in *We Didn't Mean to Go to Sea*, in which they sail unaided across the North Sea. This genuinely life-threatening adventure is immediately followed by the calmer *Secret Water* (1939). Commander Walker, their father, sets up an expedition for his children to map Hamford Water, near Walton-on-the-Naze; they encounter more local children and are joined by the Blacketts. *The Picts and the Martyrs* (1943), set the following summer, back in the Lake District, has the Great Aunt from *Swallowdale* disrupting Dick and Dorothea's visit. There are three other novels, whose 'realistic' credentials are more questionable. *Peter Duck* (1932), supposedly made up by the Swallows and the Amazons in the winter of 1930, is a pastiche of *Treasure Island* (1882), while *Missee Lee* (1941) (fictional date unknown) takes the same 'fictionalised' (or multi-fictionalised) Swallows and Amazons to the Chinese coast where they are captured by an eccentric pirate. The final book, *Great Northern* (1947), has a rather ambiguous status – neither fantasy nor reality – and takes all the children on a cruise to the Hebrides.

So, what parts of the canon appeal to me as an adult reader? Choosing my favourite chapters turned out to be remarkably easy: 'The Great Aunt Goes to See for Herself' in *The Picts and the Martyrs*, closely followed by the sequence in which two middle-class girls (daughters of a solicitor) hitch lifts across the Norfolk Broads on a series of working sailing boats in *Coot Club* ('Port and Starboard Miss their Ship,' '*Sir Garnet* Obliges Friends,' and '*Come Along* and Welcome'), and the climactic 'trial' scene, 'The Legal Mind' in *The Big Six*.

The Great Aunt's chapter is unique in the canon in that Ransome is writing exclusively about adults, and not from a child's point of view. Suspicious that her great-nieces have been visiting other children without telling her, the old(ish) lady spends an afternoon with a series of local Lake District people. The journey of the Great Aunt is for me (and this is, of course, contentious) the closest that Ransome came to writing (part of) an adult novel – and, as an adult, I think it is a superb short piece, with assured portraits of the Butcher who gives the Great Aunt a lift in his van, more concerned with his darts match, and of Mary Swainson, a local young woman:

> Mary Swainson was smiling happily when she came to the road and saw old Miss Turner, Mrs Blackett's aunt, walking towards her.
>
> Mary Swainson knew her at once. As a child she had been much in awe of her. She reminded herself that she was now grown up and was going to marry Jack, the woodman, as soon as she thought fit, while Miss Turner, poor old thing, had never

26. A Mystery Solved

married at all. Crossing the road, to go through the coppice down to her boat, she smiled at Miss Turner with a queer mixture of kindness, pity and fear.

Of course, neatly observed adults recur in the books, and, again as an adult critic, I would argue that they contribute to their depth: the laconic Doctor, *passim*, Jim Turner and his sister Molly Blackett overheard talking about her dead husband in *Swallowdale*, the monosyllabic farmer Mr Dixon and his farm-hand Silas, and the unsympathetic farmer Mrs Tyson (to whom we shall return). Of course, Jim Woodall and Simon, Old Bob, the Whittles and Mr Awkins, sailing across the Broads are always in the company of Port and Starboard and their portraits are tinged by the children's presence, but nevertheless they represent a vivid portrait of a lost way of life.

I suspect that part of my pleasure in 'The Legal Mind' is no doubt a sign of my arrested development – the unholy joy of watching George Owden (the villain) and his friend with the horrid name (as Mrs Barrable observes) get their comeuppance. Again, this is a chapter where the adult – in the person of Mr Farland, the solicitor – dominates, even though the action is largely seen and focalised through the viewpoints of the children. Tom's frustrated intervention – 'Oh, look here, Uncle Frank' (which is ignored) – merely serves to stress adult control, to which, as an adult reader, I relate instinctively. 'Mr Farland had not for nothing been a lawyer all his life' is a comment that has little for the child reader and everything for the adult reader.

But if these adults are, in the abstract, an essential part of the weft of the books, that is not to say that they are always positive for individual readings. I can still remember, as a very young reader, suddenly seeing the absorbing games played by the children in *Swallows and Amazons* in a completely new light – from the other end of the telescope, as it were. One of the farmers, 'that powerful native', Mr Jackson, at last has his say, and for a child, a rather chastising say, in the final chapter: 'Nancy wanted to empty the hay out of the haybags to make a last blaze on the camp fire. 'Nay,' said Mr Jackson, 'it's good hay that.' So it was spared to be eaten by cows.'

As an adult who has made a living from writing, and writing about writing, I also admire Ransome' technical virtuosity as a storyteller. I still read the opening chapter of *Pigeon Post* with immense pleasure, because of the dexterous way in which it foreshadows the whole of the novel – not only the pigeons, but the drought, the fell fire, the mysterious Timothy, Dick's metallurgical investigations, the pompous but effective Colonel Jolys – as well as links to the two previous years' holidays. Whatever my reservations about the first half of *We Didn't Mean to Go To Sea* (rather dull?), I find it impossible not to admire Ransome's manipulation of the folktale structure, as the children are painstakingly provided with all the skills and hardware they will need to survive the sea voyage in the second half (from the penny whistle to the translucent plates). Then there is the amazing interlocking of the final chapters of *Pigeon Post* and *The Picts and the Martyrs*, the kind of cross-cutting that, seventy years later, we have become accustomed to in sophisticated television drama.

2. Reading for my Inner Child

In agreeing to be the implied reader, we may get closest to the way in which Ransome wanted us to read – and doing so means we can be provided with some of the most intense experiences. Thus, caught willingly in the books, we can experience vividly Dick and Dorothea in the snowstorm in *Winter Holiday*, or eating through Captain Flint's stores on the *Fram*, or feel for the Walkers sailing through the storm and the night in *We Didn't Mean to Go to Sea*, or the almost ethereally dream-like sailing of 'While the Wind Holds' of *Coot Club*:

> The sun had set, the wind was dropping, but the *Teasel* was still gliding on, so smoothly, so easily, that it seemed impossible to stop. On and on they sailed. A sunset glow spread over the sky, and the reeds stood out black against it. On and on. They could hardly see where the reflections ended and the banks began. Nothing else was moving. Windmills, dark against the darkening sky, seemed twice their proper size.

It seems unlikely that many modern editors – reading as adults – would allow such a mesmerically leisurely pace into a new book – but perhaps they have forgotten how to read for their inner child-selves.

A good example of the difference between this kind of reading and an adult reading is provided by almost all of *The Big Six*. It is obvious from the fourth page who dunnit ('The only passers by who did not have a friendly word for the Death and Glories . . .'), or who is going to do it, but if we are perfect implied readers we can ignore this, and happily collude with the author and the characters' ignorance.

All of this makes for positive, involved reading, but I was interested to find there are bits of the books that my inner child does *not* want to read again; for example, Mrs Tyson being angry in *Pigeon Post* when she thinks the children have set the fell on fire: 'You've done it this time, Miss Nancy. And nowt to stop it. I should have sent you packing yesterday.'

26. A Mystery Solved

Or Dorothea using the star-book wrapper to light the fire in *Winter Holiday* (when her more outdoor-wise – and snobbish – peers would use twigs), or the reliable Captain Flint suddenly afraid in the gorge in *Missee Lee*. The experiences of the inner-child reader don't have to be all 'good'.

3. Reading for the Child I Was

It might be helpful to tell you that, from the age of around eight until about sixteen, I spent my summer holidays in the Lake District. It was, I'm almost afraid to say, in a caravan (Ransome was not fond of caravans), but in my defence (or my father's) I should say that it was only a ten-foot Eccles, and it was towed by a 1935 Riley Kestrel with a homemade dinghy on top, all of which was eccentric and authentic and probably the next best thing to being in a tent. But the key attraction about the caravan was that I had a canvas upper berth, and just at eye level was a shelf that was exactly the width of a Ransome hardback, and exactly the length of the five Lake-District novels, end to end. A really luscious symmetry, which I've probably been subconsciously searching for in shelves ever since.

We stayed first near Pooley Bridge on Ullswater, with its miniature pebble bays under the overhanging trees, and later on Windermere, where we fished early in the morning with the mist still on the water.

You might know what to expect of *my* reading for *my* past child, because, under certain circumstances, I don't actually need to open the books: it is simply enough to weigh the books with their faded green covers in my hand. It may not be surprising that *The Picts and the Martyrs* – by far the rainiest of the books – is my subconscious favourite: I can smell the damp woods and feel the lake water, whether Ransome describes them or not. As I was perhaps a bit of an outsider myself (and from a small family), Dorothea's essay at outsiderism in *Winter Holiday* speaks to me: 'She had been very happy, waking up in this new place, but those children in the boat had somehow spoilt things. A new story began to shape itself in her mind, one that nobody would be able to read without tears . . . *The Outcasts*. By Dorothea Callum.'

Old stone bridges are still etched into my psyche, and huts and farmhouses in the larch woods – places such as the old bobbin mill that as a child I remember being somewhere near Coniston (although the real landscape may have moved, as it did for Ransome). (This is all slightly confused by the fact that I read Hugh Walpole's *Rogue Herries* when I was about ten, and the only bit I understood – or remember – was the stoning of the witch at Watendlath bridge.)

Similarly, my past child relishes Susan's cooking *passim*, Dorothea's maps in Scotland Yard (Tom's garden shed in *The Big Six*), and the progressively more detailed maps in *Secret Water* – but perhaps that's enough: the children we were perhaps deserve their privacy.

4. Reading for Other Adults

Arthur Ransome, like many other children's authors, has dedicated followers, and it is not difficult to trace them if you are inclined. The books provoke ideas, or we have ideas and the books support them. Here we might be reading historically, or sociologically, or culturally: what an ideal world 1930 now seems, with so few cars, with middle-class households with nurses and cooks, and with the workers in their place – but in a *respected* place. We might be fascinated by rigging or navigation, or by recipes for cooking pemmican (aka corned beef) or the design of mowing machines. If you are me, you are interested in Ransome's expertise in folktale and narrative structures, or in arguing that his books were part of a literary fashion, or a metaphor for empire-building, or an allegory of war and impending war. We might read him to place him among his contemporaries in literature – Orwell, Lawrence, Woolf – or in children's literature – Gary Hogg, Tolkien, P.L. Travers – or to trace his political ideas. And so on. These are resilient books: they can take it. Or give it.

5. Reading on Behalf of Children

Whether we like it or not, we do this, wanting to pass on our enthusiasm and recurring delight. Mostly this reading will be the reverse of prohibitive – we might be looking for aspects of the books that might appeal to our video-game-loving son or granddaughter: perhaps swashbuckling in *Peter Duck* or an amazing female hero in *Missee Lee*. Or the appeal of ingenuity in tickling trout, building a furnace, camping, sailing a small boat – or a larger boat – or photographing rare birds.

Or we might read the books to check up on elements of the 1930s zeitgeist that are not so PC today. This might lead us to worry about sexism: one can hardly overlook the fact that Susan Walker, aka Mate Susan, is subordinate to her elder brother, Captain John. But Ransome comes off pretty well about that – or does he? Without Susan, nothing would happen, and Nancy Blackett is the natural leader (even if she seems to be trying to be a boy). Although Mrs Walker and Molly Blackett are strong and wise women, stronger men stand behind them.

26. A Mystery Solved

But that was 1930, and it may only be adult readers who are sensitive about it on behalf of the young: the proportion of stupid children is no larger than the proportion of stupid adults, and children can tell now from then, just as they can tell fantasy from reality. And so the health-and-safety readers who worry about the lack of life jackets and the sharpness of the arrows are really not worrying about anything real.

But when, or if, we wrestle with our adult power and responsibility in the face of the difference between what we make of a text and what *they*, the children of today, make of the 'same' text, it is always salutary to remember that we never know what somebody else makes of a text. Especially in the face of the five possible readings. Once you have been told that *Secret Water* is the favourite Ransome book of a fourteen-year-old girl because it, at last, shows Nancy being outed (with Daisy) then, if you are over seventy, you are henceforth more careful about making assumptions.

All of this may seem – and has been – a little self-indulgent – but it seems to me to be both practically and theoretically sound, and to be a rewarding exercise for any adult reader of Ransome – or any adult reader of any children's book.

And so, next time you are asked why you are reading a children's book . . . then the answer may take longer than the person asking expects.

Notes

1. Should Children Read Fairy Tales?

There are numerous collections of fairy tales available. A particularly attractive one is *The Classic Fairy Tales*, edited with illustrations and useful commentaries by Iona and Peter Opie (Oxford University Press, 1974). Bruno Bettelheim's famous but much-disputed interpretation of fairy tales is *The Uses of Enchantment; the Meaning and Importance of Fairy Tales* (Vintage Books, 1989). The controversies about fairy stories are discussed particularly in *Suitable for Children? Controversies in Children's Literature* by Nicholas Tucker (Sussex University Press, 1976).

2. What Makes a Children's Classic?

Recent discussion on the 'classic' can be found in *The Cambridge Companion to Children's Literature* (Cambridge University Press, 2009), *Modern Children's Literature: An Introduction* (Palgrave, 2014), and *Canon Constitution and Canon Change in Children's Literature* (Routledge, 2017).

3. Why Were there no Nursery Rhymes before 1744?

The many collections of nursery rhymes are often superbly illustrated, such as *Lavender Blue*, edited by Kathleen Lines and illustrated by Harold Jones (Oxford University Press, 1954). The best scholarly edition is *The Oxford Dictionary of Nursery Rhymes*, edited by Iona and Peter Opie (Oxford

University Press, new edition 1997). *Tom Thumb's Pretty Song Book, Vol. II*, has been magnificently reprinted by the Cotsen Family Foundation, edited by Andrea Immel and Brian Alderson in 2013.

4. Who Wrote Little Goody Two-Shoes?

The most recent edition of *Little Goody Two-Shoes* can be found in *Little Goody Two-Shoes and Other Stories; Originally Published by John Newbery*, edited by M.O. Grenby (Palgrave, 2013). John Newbery's *A Little Pretty Pocket-Book* was reprinted by Oxford University Press in 1966.

5. What (and Where) Are the Secret, Lost Books of Childhood – and Why Do they Matter?

Alison Waller has recently published *Rereading Childhood Books*, a study of how adults revisit, remember, and forget children's books that were significant to them (Bloomsbury, 2019).

6. The Curious History of Three Bears . . . and a Lamb

'The Three Bears' and 'Scrapefoot' can be found in *English Fairy Tales*, collected by Joseph Jacobs (Bodley Head, 1984). 'The Three Bears' is discussed in F.J. Harvey Darton's *Children's Books in England* (Cambridge University Press, 1982), and the controversial history of 'Mary Had a Little Lamb' is discussed by Iona and Peter Opie in *The Oxford Dictionary of Nursery Rhymes*.

7. Charles Kingsley: Christian Socialist, Evangelical Storyteller, or Sexual Sadist?

The best edition of *The Water-Babies* is edited by Brian Alderson (Oxford World's Classics, 1995). Kingsley's life and psychology are discussed in Humphrey Carpenter's *Secret Gardens* (Allen and Unwin, 1985) and Susan Chitty's *The Beast and the Monk: A Life of Charles Kingsley* (Hodder and Stoughton, 1974).

8. Who Was the Real William Brighty Rands?

There are no recent editions of the poetry of William Brightly Rands, but selections may be found in such anthologies as *The Oxford Book of Children's Verse*, edited by Iona and Peter Opie (Oxford University Press, 1973). A CD of twenty-four 'Lilliput Lyrics' was produced by his great-grandson David Rands in 2005.

10. Was Lorna Doone really Married?

The best recent edition of *Lorna Doone* is edited by Sally Shuttleworth (Oxford World's Classics, 1994).

11. Whatever Happened to God in Children's Books?

An earlier version of this essay appeared as 'The Loss of the Father and the Loss of God in English-Language Children's Literature (1800-2000)' in *Religion, Children's Literature and Modernity in Western Europe 1750-2000* (Leuven University Press, 2005).

12. Whose Side Was Henty really on in the American Civil War?

Second-hand copies of G.A. Henty's books can still be found fairly easily. Henty's friend G. Manville Fenn wrote a dull biography *George Alfred Henty: The Story of an Active Life* (Blackie, 1902), and there is a more literary survey by Guy Arnold, *Held Fast for England: G.A. Henty: Imperialist Boys' Writer* (Hamish Hamilton, 1980).

13. What Do Children's Books Do about Christmas?

This essay is based on talks given at the Christmas Children's Literature Festival at Università degli Studi Suor Orsola Benincasa, Napoli. I am very grateful to Professor Stefania Tondo for her encouragement and hospitality.

14. Is Little Lord Fauntleroy a Children's Story – and Does the Subplot work?

The best recent edition of *Little Lord Fauntleroy* is edited by Dennis Butts (Oxford World's Classics, 1993). The standard biography is *Waiting for the Party: The Life of Frances Hodgson Burnett, 1849-1924*, by Ann Thwaite (Secker and Warburg, 1974).

15. Why Was Billy Bunter never really Expelled from Greyfriars School?

Most of the stories about Billy Bunter and Greyfriars School have been reprinted in book form by Howard Baker in ten volumes of *Magnet* facsimiles. (Howard Baker, 1969-91). *The Autobiography of Frank Richards* was reprinted in a 'Memorial Edition' (Charles Skilton, 1962); the best literary study is *Frank Richards: the Chap behind the Chums* by Mary Cadogan (Viking, 1988).

16. Why on Earth Are there Children's Books about War?

An earlier version of this essay appeared as 'War in Children's Literature – Why?' in *Mundos en Conflicto: Representación de Ideologías, Enfrentamientos Sociales y Guerras en la Literatura Infantil y Juvenil*, Universidade de Vigo, in 2005.

17. Biggles: Tough Guy or Romantic Hero?

Many of W.E. Johns's stories about Biggles are in print, and others are easily found second-hand. Peter Berresford Ellis and Jennifer Schofield have written an excellent biography – *Biggles! The Life Story of Capt W.E. Johns: Creator of Biggles, Worrals, Gimlet & Steeley* (Veloce Publishing, 1993).

18. Why Is there Nobody Nice at St Clare's?

The girls' school story has had a great deal of expert scholarship devoted to it. Mary Cadogan and Patricia Craig's pioneering *You're a Brick, Angela! The Girls' Story 1839-1985* (Gollancz, 1986) remains authoritative and highly readable. The definitive scholarly work on Enid Blyton is David Rudd's *Enid Blyton and the Mystery of Children's Literature* (Macmillan, 2000).

19. Were there Two Flutes? Time Present and Time Past at Green Knowe

The first five of Lucy Boston's stories about Green Knowe are published by Faber & Faber. Her two volumes of autobiography, including much information about her famous house and garden, the Manor at Hemingford Grey, have been collectively reprinted as *Memories* (Colt Books, 1992). Jasper Rose published a short critical study, *Lucy Boston* (Bodley Head, 1965).

20. Why Does C.S. Lewis Annoy so many People?

Lewis's essays are collected in *Of Other Worlds* (reissued, Harper, 2017); Rowan Williams's *The Lion's World: A Journey into the Heart of Narnia* is published by SPCK (2012).

21. What Happened Next? The Problem of Sequels

Further information about inconsistencies in the William books and Malcolm Saville's Lone Pine stories can be found in Mary Cadogan's *Richmal Crompton: The Woman behind William* (Allen and Unwin, 1986) and *The Complete Lone Pine: The 'Lone Pine' Books of Malcolm Saville* (Mark O'Hanlon, 1996).

22. To See Ourselves . . . What Image of the British Do Children's Books Give the World?

This essay is based on a research project on comparative children's literature undertaken with Professor Laura Tosi of Università Ca' Foscari, Venice. I am very grateful for her permission to use this material, which she has developed in *The Fabulous Journeys of Alice and Pinocchio* (McFarland, 2018).

23. Why Is there no such Thing as Children's Poetry?

Excellent discussions of children's poetry can be found in *Poetry for Children: The Signal Award 1979-2001*, edited by Nancy Chambers (Thimble Press, 2009), and *Poetry and Childhood,* edited by Morag Styles, Louise Joy, and David Whitley, (Trentham Books, 2010). The best history of British children's poetry is *From the Garden to the Street* by Morag Styles (Cassell, 1998).

24. Which Are the Best 100 Children's Books?

One Hundred Books Famous in Children's Literature was published by the Grolier Club (2014). C.M. Yonge's *What Books to Lend and What to Give* was published by the National Society's Depository (1887).

25. And Which Is the Best?

A wide-ranging list and discussion of children's book prizes can be found in Ruth Allen's *Winning Books* (Pied Piper, 2005).

26. A Mystery Solved: How Adults Read Children's Books

An earlier version of this essay appeared in *Mixed Moss*, the journal of the Arthur Ransome Society.

Index of Author Names

Abbott, Joseph, 116
Adams, Richard, 141
Aesop, 14
Ahlberg, Janet and Allan, 71
Alcott, Louisa May, 11, 58-9, 77, 114, 119
Allen, Nicholas, 71, 72
Almond, David, 141
Andersen, Hans Christian, 1, 3, 4, 138
Anderson, Rachel, 88
Ardizzone, Edward, 84
Atkinson, M.E., 10
Ballantyne, R.M., 138
Banks, Lynne Reid, 88
Barrie, J.M., 48, 126
Baugh, Helen, 71
Baum, L. Frank, 49, 136
Bawden, Nina, 48
Beck, Ian, 72
Belloc, Hilaire, 43
Bemelmans, Ludwig, 123
Blackmore, R.D., 52-5
Blake, Quentin, 72
Blake, William, 43
Blume, Judy, 136
Blyton, Enid, 11, 24, 28, 30, 46, 71, 94, 96-100, 112, 136, 141, 143

Boreman, Thomas, 14
Boston, Lucy M., 50, 101-5
Brent-Dyer, Elinor, 46
Bridges, Robert, 130
Briggs, Raymond, 70
Brisley, Joyce Lankester, 27-8
Brooks, Kevin, 51, 142
Browne, Anthony, 136
Buchanan, George, 72
Buckeridge, Anthony, 116, 117-8
Bunyan, John, 138
Burgess, Anna, 134
Burgess, Melvin, 136
Burnett, Francis Hodgson, 10, 47, 49, 74-8, 114
Cannan, Joanna, 10
Carey, Mariah, 71
Carle, Eric, 136
Carroll, Lewis, 11, 77, 121, 126, 136
Chambers, Aidan, 60
Charlesworth, Maria Louisa, 59
Collington, Peter, 72
Collodi, Carlo, 122, 125, 126
Cominius, John Amos, 136
Conan Doyle, Arthur, 119
Cooper, J. Fenimore, 116
Cooper, Mary, 13, 14-15

Cote, Jenny L., 61-2
Crompton, Richmal, 118, 124
Cross, Gillian, 58, 86
Cundall, Joseph, 32
Curtis, Richard, 71
Dahl, Roald, 24, 50-1, 141, 143
De Amicis, Edmondo, 126
de Brunhoff, Jean, 48, 122
Delderfield, R.F., 117
de Selincourt, Aubrey, 109
de Witt, Cornelius, 26
Dickens, Charles, 4-5, 70, 78
Disney, Walt, 4, 122, 126
Donaldson, Julia, 73
Drinkwater, John, 130
Edgeworth, Maria, 3, 138
Ende, Michael, 123
Faulkner, J. Meade, 49
Fletcher, Tom, 71
Fine, Anne, 50, 86
Foreman, Michael, 73
Fuller, Roy, 129
Gaiman, Neil, 48, 51
Gardner, Sally, 51
Garner, Alan, 141
Gaskell, Elizabeth, 138
Gay, John, 14
Goodrich, Samuel (see Parley, Peter)
Goldsmith, Oliver, 20-1
Grahame, Kenneth, 8, 72-3, 117, 126
Grey, Andrew, 71
Grimm, Jacob and Wilhelm, 1, 3, 4, 123, 138
Hale, Sarah Josepha, 32, 33-4
Henty, G.A., 63-7
Hardinge, Frances, 147
Hargreaves, Roger, 11, 71
Hoban, Russell, 166, 139
Hoffman, Heinrich, 123
Hofland, Barbara, 138
Hogg, Garry, 10, 154
Horne, Richard, 70
Horowitz, Anthony, 51, 144
Horse, Harry (see Richard Horne)
Horwood, William, 117
Hughes, Shirley, 71
Hughes, Ted, 132-3

Hughes, Thomas, 10
Hunter, Sally, 71
Hutchins, Pat, 71
Impey, Martin, 73
Jacobs, Joseph, 31
Janeway, James, 14
Jansson, Tove, 124-5
Johns, W.E., 11, 91-3, 117
Johnson, Joyce A., 28, 29
Jones, Griffith and Giles, 20
Kästner, Erich, 123
Kerr, Judith, 71
Kimmell, Eric, 86
Kingsley, Charles, 35-9
Larom, Betty, 25, 30
Landman, Tanya, 51
Lear, Edward, 43
Leeson, Robert, 117
Le Guin, Ursula K., 87
Lewis, C.S., 48, 56, 60, 61, 73, 99, 106-113, 114, 141, 146
Lindgren, Astrid, 49, 122, 124
Lindstrom, Eric, 51
Lovelace, Maud Hart, 96
MacCaughrean, Geraldine, 72
MacDonald, George, 42, 138
Magorian, Michelle, 48
Mantle, Ben, 71
Mark, Jan, 128, 129
Marryat, Captain Frederick, 10, 138
Martineau, Harriet, 10
Masefield, John, 60, 136
May, Robert L., 70
Milne, A.A., 48, 71, 126, 129-30
Montgomery, L.M., 49
Moore, Clement Clarke, 68, 70
Morpurgo, Michael, 71, 72, 73, 86
Morse, Brian, 129
Moss, Miriam, 86
Motion, Andrew, 117
Mure, Eleanor, 31-2
Needle, Jan, 117
Nesbit, Edith, 49, 117
Ness, Patrick, 51
Newbery, John, 15, 18, 19, 21
Norton, Mary, 114
Osmond, Edward, 143

Parley, Peter, 115, 116
Parsons, Garry, 71
Pausewang, Gudrun, 86
Pearce, Philippa, 141
Perrault, Charles, 1, 3, 14, 15, 136
Peters, Jan, 72
Peyton, K.M., 119, 142
Porter, Eleanor H., 49
Potter, Beatrix, 11, 48, 71, 127
Poynter, Dougie, 71
Pratchett, Terry, 89
Pullman, Philip, 61, 109, 141, 144
Quiller-Couch, Arthur, 117
Rands, William Brighty, 40-45
Ransome, Arthur, 10, 46, 50, 60, 141, 147-55
Reade, Charles, 52
Richards, Frank, 79-83, 95
Richards, Kel, 52
Robinson, Hilary, 73
Rosen, Michael, 131-2
Rowling, J.K., 24, 50, 58, 61, 73, 77, 114, 122, 136, 144
Saunders, Kate, 117
Saville, Malcolm, 118
Savit, Gavriel, 86
Sawyer, Mary, 32-4
Scannel, Vernon, 129
Scarry, Richard, 71
Seuss, Dr, 70
Severn, David, 10
Shakespeare, William, 78
Sherwood, Martha Mary, 38, 56, 58, 136

Southey, Robert, 31
Spyri, Johanna, 9, 49, 123
Stanley, Mandy, 71
Stevenson, Robert Louis, 11, 44, 114, 116-7, 138
Streatfeild, Noel, 49-50
Stoor, Catherine, 72
Stratemeyer, Edward, 116
Sullivan, Deirdre, 58
Thomas, Dylan, 129
Thompson, Emma, 71
Titus, Eve, 122-3
Tocsvig, Sandi, 86
Tolkien, J.R.R., 88, 109, 154
Tozer, Katharine, 28-30
Travers, P.L., 126, 154
Trimmer, Sarah, 3-4, 136-7
Turner, Ethel M., 57, 59-60
'TW', 14
Twain, Mark, 49, 119, 122, 124
Vallance, Rosalind, 26-8, 29
Vincent, Gabrielle, 122, 123
Vivas, Julie, 72
Waddell, Martin, 72
Watts, Isaac, 138
Westall, Robert, 86, 141
Westerman, Percy F., 85, 86
Wibberley, Leonard, 117
Wilder, Laura Ingalls, 96, 124
Wildsmith, Brian, 72
Williams, Ursula Moray, 28
Wilson, Jacqueline, 50
Yonge, Charlotte M., 20, 138

You may also be interested in:

How Did Long John Silver Lose his Leg?
and Twenty-Six Other Mysteries of Children's Literature

by Dennis Butts and Peter Hunt

A wide-ranging and lively exploration of the questions raised by the classics of children's fiction, in the texts themselves and in their cultural reception.

How did Long John Silver Lose His Leg? is a wonderfully diverting tour through some of the best-loved classics of children's literature, addressing many of the unanswered questions that inspire intense speculation when the books are laid down.

Could Bobbie's train really have stopped in time (*The Railway Children*)? Did Beatrix Potter have the 'flu in 1909, and did this lead to a certain darkness in her work (*The Tale of Mr Tod*)? Would the 'rugby football' played by Tom Brown be recognised by sportsmen today (*Tom Brown's Schooldays*)? Having established the cultural importance of children's books in the modern age, the authors also consider the more serious issues posed by the genre. Why are we so defensive of the idyllic worlds presented in children's books? Why have some of our best-loved authors been outed as neglectful parents to their own children? Should we ever separate the book from its creator and appreciate the works of writers convicted of crimes against children?

A treat for any enthusiast of children's literature, this entertaining book provides rich detail, witty explication, and serious food for thought.

234x156mm / 154pp / Illustrations: b&w / Published: 2013
Paperback ISBN: 978 0 7188 9310 1 / ePDF ISBN: 978 0 7188 4193 5
ePub ISBN: 978 0 7188 4194 2 / Kindle ISBN: 978 0 7188 4195 9

You may also be interested in:

Children's Literature and Social Change
Some Case Studies from Barbara Hofland to Philip Pullman

by Dennis Butts

Twelve innovative case studies covering the period from the early 19th century, exploring children's literature in its social, cultural and political context.

While there are many books about children's literature, few discuss it within its social context or investigate the ways writers reflect or react to change in society. Dennis Butts explores how shifting attitudes and historical upheavals from the 1840s onwards affected and continue to affect books written for younger audiences.

234x156mm / 208pp / Published: 2010 / Paperback ISBN: 978 0 7188 9208 1

From the Dairyman's Daughter to Worrals of the WAAF
The RTS, Lutterworth Press and Children's Literature

by Dennis Butts and Pat Garrett (editors)

Essays analysing the development of 18th-20th century children's literature, and the role played by the Religious Tract Society and the Lutterworth Press.

A collection of essays based on the Children's Books History Society study conference marking the bicentenary of the Religious Tract Society and the Lutterworth Press. The book analyses the children's literature it produced, charting the development of the genre from the evangelical tract through to the popular school story. The work studies the two great magazines for which the RTS and Lutterworth were known to generations of children as well as other magazines.

234x156mm / 256pp / Published: 2006 / Paperback ISBN: 978 0 7188 3055 7